Devil's Advocates

DEVIL'S ADVOCATES is a series of books devoted to exploring the classics of horror cinema. Contributors to the series come from the fields of teaching, academia, journalism and fiction, but all have one thing in common: a passion for the horror film and a desire to share it with the widest possible audience.

'The admirable Devil's Advocates series is not only essential – and fun – reading for the serious horror fan but should be set texts on any genre course.'
Dr Ian Hunter, Reader in Film Studies, De Montfort University, Leicester

'Auteur Publishing's new Devil's Advocates critiques on individual titles... offer bracingly fresh perspectives from passionate writers. The series will perfectly complement the BFI archive volumes.' **Christopher Fowler,** *Independent on Sunday*

'Devil's Advocates has proven itself more than capable of producing impassioned, intelligent analyses of genre cinema... quickly becoming the go-to guys for intelligent, easily digestible film criticism.' **Horror Talk.com**

'Auteur Publishing continue the good work of giving serious critical attention to significant horror films.' **Black Static**

 DevilsAdvocatesbooks

DevilsAdBooks

ALSO AVAILABLE IN THIS SERIES

A Girl Walks Home Alone at Night Farshid Kazemi

Black Sunday Martyn Conterio

The Blair Witch Project Peter Turner

Blood and Black Lace Roberto Curti

The Blood on Satan's Claw David Evans-Powell

Candyman Jon Towlson

Cannibal Holocaust Calum Waddell

Cape Fear Rob Daniel

Carrie Neil Mitchell

The Company of Wolves James Gracey

The Conjuring Kevin Wetmore

Creepshow Simon Brown

Cruising Eugenio Ercolani & Marcus Stiglegger

The Curse of Frankenstein Marcus K. Harmes

Daughters of Darkness Kat Ellinger

Dead of Night Jez Conolly & David Bates

The Descent James Marriot

The Devils Darren Arnold

Don't Look Now Jessica Gildersleeve

The Evil Dead Lloyd Haynes

The Fly Emma Westwood

Frenzy Ian Cooper

Halloween Murray Leeder

House of Usher Evert Jan van Leeuwen

In the Mouth of Madness Michael Blyth

It Follows Joshua Grimm

Ju-on The Grudge Marisa Hayes

Let the Right One In Anne Billson

M Samm Deighan

Macbeth Rebekah Owens

The Mummy Doris V. Sutherland

Nosferatu Cristina Massaccesi

Peeping Tom Kiri Bloom Walden

Prevenge Andrew Graves

Re-Animator Eddie Falvey

Repulsion Jeremy Carr

Saw Benjamin Poole

Scream Steven West

The Shining Laura Mee

Shivers Luke Aspell

The Silence of the Lambs Barry Forshaw

Suspiria Alexandra Heller-Nicholas

The Texas Chain Saw Massacre James Rose

The Thing Jez Conolly

Trouble Every Day Kate Robertson

Twin Peaks: Fire Walk With Me Lindsay Hallam

The Witch Brandon Grafius

Witchfinder General Ian Cooper

FORTHCOMING

[REC] Jim Harper

Possession Alison Taylor

Snuff Mark McKenna

DEVIL'S ADVOCATES

SCROOGE

COLIN FLEMING

Acknowledgements

The person who deserves singling out with this project is my editor, John Atkinson, the erudite and efficient good soul who presides over this series of dark works which I think, paradoxically, bring a lot of light into the world. There was a time when horror films weren't taken seriously as art. Maybe that time still persists, but John's efforts on behalf of the Devil's Advocates books, and on behalf of his writers, makes me believe that there's less of that attitude than previously, which is a great thing in a world that, alas, carries within it a real degree of its own form of darkness. In my passionate view, little is able to mitigate darkness like a horror film can. It is a special irony of the best of them, which you are well aware, if you have horror films that you love.

There are certain subjects in my writing career that I feel more indebted to than others. *Scrooge* is certainly one of them. It's a film that has given me much, and in some ways, I think it's still in the early portion of its generous bequeathing. For that is how much it touches me anew each time I watch it, and I think it always will, more so the next time than the last time. Until my own last time, I suppose.

First published in 2021 by
Auteur, an imprint of
Liverpool University Press,
4 Cambridge Street,
Liverpool
L69 7ZU

Series design: Nikki Hamlett at Cassels Design
Set by Cassels Design, Luton UK

All rights reserved. No part of this publication may be reproduced in any material form (including photocopying or storing in any medium by electronic means and whether or not transiently or incidentally to some other use of this publication) without the permission of the copyright owner.

All figures from *Scrooge* © George Minter Productions

British Library Cataloguing-in-Publication Data
A catalogue record for this book is available from the British Library

ISBN paperback: 978-1-80085-704-9
ISBN hardback: 978-1-80085-703-2
ISBN epub: 978-1-80085-830-5
ISBN PDF: 978-1-80085-748-3

Contents

A few prefatory remarks from a hooded host, who is himself hosted 7

Reel I: Opening Visitation 11

Reel II: Curse of the Stand-Alone Miser 25

Reel III: Tickled Bleak 35

Reel IV: House of Scrooge 49

Reel V: Them Scrooge Eyes 59

Reel VI: This Glowing Hand 67

Reel VII: Un-Oozy 83

Reel VIII: He Returneth and He Danceth By 101

A FEW PREFATORY REMARKS FROM A HOODED HOST, WHO IS HIMSELF HOSTED

I think any horror film fan can agree that for an undertaking of cinematic terror to work, it has to find a way to get at us. That's not the same, certainly, as appearing in front of our faces. We need to be at a place and time in our lives where a film, if it's formidable enough, can all but reach out and say, "I got you now!" We are taken, we are terrified, and we welcome that taking and that terror, because we feel so alive. Even when we're dealing with the dead. Or the dead are dealing with us, as it were.

I think that's one of the great paradoxical powers of the horror film. The charnel house opens us up to new, verdant worlds within ourselves. We may question the nature of what it means to be dead, if the bogeys and the haunts of our favorite horror films have this life-spreading knack. We question, and we affirm. We challenge by being challenged, and we realize by dint of knowing, and conceivably newly knowing, what it means to be alive, which often times has little to do with "mere" respiration and pulse beat.

In my experience, people who love horror films are some of the most alive people I know. They are not necessarily children, and they may be wise and mature, but they retain the child's capacity for wonder. An adult with said capacity is an impressive being, in my view. Equipped to face the trials of life with energy, creative problem skills. A saving sense of humor, despite macabre goings-on, which would thrill a horror film director like James Whale, who understood the art—and the necessity—of both laughing as one passed the proverbial graveyard, but also recognizing the gravity all but saturating the air.

The finest horror films—like the finest art of any stripe—are those that corner and catch us most readily, in the various spurts, stages, iterations of our lives. And who we are. As adults we'll watch the B-grade sci-fi horror effort that thrilled us as a child of thirteen, with that pleasing infusion of nostalgia that makes us feel safe when we recall what once frightened us so much. We'll want to share that film with our own kids. But that's not the same as the horror film that is experienced as deeply, but differently, at all of the spurts, stages, iterations of our lives. Their artistry of terror has a built-in malleability, just as conceivably the human soul does. I always imagine these films in effect saying to us, "Ready when you are," to bend once more to whom we've become, or maybe bend us a little, too, to whom we might better become.

Scrooge (1951), as you will read in these pages, has always been that film for me, I think: more than any movie, not just a horror movie. Make no mistake about it: a story about a guy who is totally alone, with no love, no friends, who lives in what looks like a haunted house, in this 1951 version, and then becomes a literal haunted house, who is shown—by no less than four ghosts—the most painful aspects of his life, his memories, and his non-existent prospects—that is, his complete absence of hope as he is currently constituted—is one mighty matzo ball of horror. It borders on the overwhelming. No wonder the film appeared for so long primarily on late night TV schedules, when gentle folk, as the saying goes, ought to have been asleep.

The film is much else besides, but the substrate of horror is always the surface upon which our carriage rattles down (until, mercifully, the terror breaks with a joy that, to me, is beyond even Handel's "Hallelujah" chorus in *Messiah*) in the lonely dead of this night, as though we were advancing upon Castle Dracula, save that this is a House of Scrooge. It could well double as the figurative house of all of us, too, in some part, be that part a mountain-sized chunk, or a sliver that could fit between the pages of a book.

If you've read Charles Dickens' 1843 novella *A Christmas Carol*, you know that there is a lightness at times to the tone. You'll experience it also in scores and scads of seasonal theatrical productions, from those mounted by local high school kids to the big city staple that has run at the same theater for thirty years. That wit is provided by the third-person narrator. He is an imp. Not a literal imp, though I guess he also might be. We don't really know.

In the 1951 film, there's humor, but it comes in other ways. Alastair Sim, as Scrooge, is responsible for what there is of it. His humor, though, is also plaintive. It's head-shaking humor. We laugh, but it's with the noggin moving from side to side in a gesture of passed judgment—for after all, we are only human—and empathy. *That* kind of humor.

But what I always liked about the book—which I think is a perfect work of art (though I believe—I truly do—that this film is the greater work of art)—is how that narrator addresses each of us specifically—or that's how it feels—with that line about standing in the space of the crook of your elbow. Right next to you. All along. And you didn't notice it until just then. If you're like me, you might even stop reading at that point, and take a quick look around you. I love that quick look. I live for things like that quick look.

I wanted to channel my version of that spirit in walking alongside of you with this book. I'm the ghost of the authorial present. Or the near future, I suppose, as soon as our time together officially starts when you move out of this preface and we begin our shared journey through this film, and also a sort of film-beyond-the-film. The nimbus of the film. The penumbra of the film. Pick what term you like. Because a true work of art always goes, and takes us, beyond itself, in a sense.

When we are grabbed by a horror film, we feel that we've been solely clutched. The experience is so personal. And yet, many others have this same experience, each in their way, and the personal and the universal enter into a dialogue we may not be aware of—thus is the intensity of our own experience—until we take a few paces back, and let our senses, and our minds, utilize a different kind of deep focus than we get with some of the cinematography in *Scrooge*, which we'll also inspect on our particular dissecting table.

So I'm going to invite you, at times, into the crook of my own elbow, where you are perhaps already standing, as if waiting for me, and I'll tell you about the universal ways that this film got at me as an individual. Because I think that's what matters, what allows a work like *Scrooge* to get discovered, rediscovered, loved, loved anew, and for it to do what it can for us, and those we care about, those we don't know, and, dare I say it, the world out there of viewers who prosper by being haunted by this film, each in their own way, one that is also, in sublime and beautiful ways, the ways of all of us.

I am in loose-hanging, over-big sweatshirt as I write these words, with the hood over my head for warmth. It is dark outside, there is a mug of spiced tea beside me on the desk. I'm thinking of what it means to simultaneously occupy the past, the present, and the future. And now I am ready for a journey into, through, around, and inside of a film.

This would be the part where I solemnly intone, "Touch the sleeve of my hoodie, and away we go!"

Let's all be in the crooks of each other's elbows. And let's let *Scrooge* get at all of us, in what, I hope, is a new way for every one, in the words of one boy who lived after all, from another boy, who is now a man, who was inspired to.

Reel 1: Opening Visitation

Were someone to ask me if ghosts were real, I would say yes, because humans are real, and I don't believe we get to a point of realness without a nudge from that which haunts us.

Say the word "ghost," and you conjure up notions of the boogity-boogity, vaporous specters like those we know from our earliest childhood recollections of Disney short films such as 1937's *Lonesome Ghosts*, in which a pack of spirits, bored and lacking anyone to haunt, dupe Mickey Mouse and his pals into a psychical investigation, just so they have someone to frighten.

But the truth is, in real life, back to our earliest days of primitive humanity when scratches on cave walls were made by one individual to show another individual what was the stuff of their nightmares, we've never been lonesome for ghosts—not if we truly understand the nature of these entities (or non-entities), as Charles Dickens understood them, and as some filmmakers who would follow him a century later did as well.

As a young boy, I was terrified of the dark, which was incongruous with my love of all things horror. Not grisly, chainsaw-based horror, but the horror that emanates in forms just-ever-so-slightly beyond our normal, natural ken, and makes shadow-bathed inroads into the very core of who we are. Who we think are. What we had determined, previously, that we knew, and which we now might need to reconsider. Before—and this was the part I liked best—it is too late. Horror put you on the clock.

The best works of terror often have that built-in time component, a stressed accent of the temporal and a keening, warning voice of, "You better remedy what needs remedying, because it's already gobbling up who you are."

Shakespeare's Lear utters his cry of "Oh, untimely death" because he realizes a loophole of salvation has closed before he could step free of the bite. Artful horror is deeply humanistic, a fair-play mystery of the self where we have a say in our development, the epiphanies we might embrace, rather than seek an escape from, as we did previously. Horror can be a damn fine friend. So long as you also give your friend some space, lest he end your mortal life or snatch away your soul, though I think this is something we can also be complicit in on our own, with the way we go about our lives on autopilot. Sometimes horror is adept at taking the reins when we most need another driver for our phantom carriage.

I'd spent early winter afternoons in the basement of the local library, which was known as the kids' level, a label I found ironic, like I was privy to a subterranean secret lair that no adult had direct access to, and that was vaguely hell-ish. After all, you were in the earth, or under the surface of the ground, anyway.

There were hordes of books on horror films, with stills from the early Universal classics like 1931's *Dracula* and *Frankenstein*, the latter movie rammed with German Expressionistic hallmarks that I couldn't identify as such at the time, but which made the pictures extra-eldritch, if you will, to me, and provided the same piquant thrill that my favorite time of the year did as well—that stretch from mid-October to Christmas—when the days became ever shorter.

I'd lose myself in a corner nook for hours, my only thought as per the outside world being that my mother had similarly lost herself upstairs in an Agatha Christie mystery, as if there were some rule that we had to down the entire contents of several volumes before we'd be allowed to check out others and tote them home.

But at night, in my room, my fears overwhelmed me. The very bed overwhelmed me. I viewed it as a prospective final resting place in this home where I had come to live, with these parents with whom I had not began my life.

My origins were something rather Dickensian, involving a fifteen-year-old biological mother who was impregnated by a married roué with a couple kids of his own. "We" began in New Bedford, not far from where Herman Melville lit out to sea on the voyage that would inform his own slant on horror in *Moby-Dick* (1851), a terror tale of psychological torment and the self-haunting nature of obsession, which would later cause its author to tell his buddy Nathaniel Hawthorne—an ace man of horror himself—that he had written an evil book, and God help his soul.

On account of the shame—for my in utero self represented a stigmata of sorts for an arch Catholic family—we were shipped off to Cape Cod, where I was born on a boat—goodness knows what was going on—and then given up, mother and child returning to New Bedford separately, she to her family, me to a foster home, once again near the dock where the *Acushnet* had carried Mr. Melville off to sea.

After a short passage of time, I was adopted, but the idea that I could be given up, cast aside—the same fear that we will observe dogging Alastair Sim's Ebenezer Scrooge in the film that has meant the most to my life—roiled my insides at night in the bed. I'd think, "well, it might be a different pillow tomorrow, somewhere else," and so I'd have to plead with my parents to let me lay down in a Spider-man sleeping bag in the room just off of the one where they sat on the couch, watching a Boston Bruins hockey game or an episode of *Dallas*. I felt safe, and would not awake as my father carried me up the stairs when the time had come.

Which is also how I felt on December afternoons in the basement of the public library, looking at those stills of Bela Lugosi, Boris Karloff, Werner Krauss in *The Cabinet of Dr. Caligari* (1920), a work that would smudge its visual thumbprints all over the one masterpiece that director Brian Desmond Hurst was ever to make, a picture I feel—even leaving aside my own connection to it—is the richest, most rewarding, surprising work of cinematic horror that we have. A film to truly change a person's life, if they gave themselves over to its darkness.

There had already been the list for Santa, and now that sweet, nuzzling feeling of anticipation and hope, to paraphrase a line of James Joyce's, was general all over my small province of childhood. But something had happened one year, during the season of Yule, with my beloved ghosts and monsters already on my mind—my Christmas wish list was topped with requests for those plastic Remco figures of the original Universal run—that led to one of the most powerful artistic discoveries I'd ever have, come the next year's Noel.

Two sisters—twins—had also been adopted into my family after me, and for a time, I had siblings, until their biological mother took them back, which was apparently something that could be done in those days. I became a child terrified of adults and what they could do in that "cruel world" that young Scrooge references to young Marley, with its vicissitudes of caprice and power.

I withdrew. I stopped talking. I doubled down in my intense need to be in that Spider-man sleeping bag away from my own room and bed. But now when my father carried me back upstairs as my parents themselves retired for the evening, I only pretended to be asleep, because my defenses were up, and I did not know where I might reside by the end of the week. Or the morrow. Outside. In another home. With new parents. Back where I had begun, perhaps, unwanted in New Bedford.

I was a little version of Sim's Scrooge, particularly that iteration of him that features only in the "extra" material that writer Noel Langley put into the script of the film that is our subject; that is, a fleshing out of Scrooge's early days in business which Dickens himself had not provided, when Ebenezer lost his ability to trust anyone in the world—even those who loved him. That is true horror. Because it is intrinsically, and intricately, human. The bogey of the self. He has a genius, it would appear, for always being there.

My mother and I were close, in part because of our love for books. Even when I could not read, I loved books. I literally pressed them to my chest, as if my heart, and where I figured my soul was, hanging there all invisible, could in this fashion best absorb their contents. A version of that same fusion that Dickens espoused, and, I think, Sim's Scrooge in particular, with greater believability, with the mastery of blending past, present, and future at once. One is fully present in one's moment, but cognizant of what has been, and focused on finding the ultimate in what will be. We occupy multiple temporal planes at once, whether we wish to or not. How we budget what gets the most of our attention will determine a portion of the quality of our lives. The past will eat you alive if you stay within it too long. The future can frighten you into dormancy before it has happened. The present is often the lynchpin. It's home row, for any old school typists out there. It's our base. And it must be well-maintained, because it helps in understanding that which is already over and done, and it can help us help ourselves for what follows.

I say that Sim's Scrooge is more believable, because in *A Christmas Carol*, Dickens' beloved 1843 tome, there is an emphasis on charm, whimsy, wonder. The narrative voice is your guide to this world of the spirits that move among men, and one man most in particular, but we never sense what I call the necromancer's art, the trip to the graveyard, for information, that might not have the return trip home. The prospect of the final, doomed stay. Perpetual residence in darkness. The lost self that is now central to our age of social media "likes," with ginned up attempts at the procurement of attention, and the putting forward of a stage act that belies, and desiccates, the true person inside.

Fifty years after the publication of Dickens' "pleasing terror," to use a phrase by M.R. James, who would exhibit his own bent for horror stories during Christmastide, and some sixty years before the Halloween 1951 release—and make no mistake about the meaning behind that date—of Hurst's *Scrooge* (retitled *A Christmas Carol* for the American market, undercutting a part of the film's thematic thrust from the jump), British author Edith Nesbit penned one of our dozen best horror stories in "Man-Size in Marble" (1887), a work ultimately about the stony ossification of the human soul. The tale involves a cottage built on ruins, where dead knights come back to life, having at a protagonist who disregards a vital warning. It's not hard to read the story and think of Alastair Sim's Scrooge as that character, without the willingness to be haunted, in the positive way which he ultimately is. How differently his night of terror could have gone. But the theme of man-as-stone resonates, and it's the kind of English horror that gets built upon by those seeking not merely to scare, but also to edify. To provide a service. A "Man-Size in Marble" is part of the English tradition of the scare story; whereas, Scrooge doubles as a service work. It's a new type of British movie terror.

Hurst, Langley, Sim, and cinematographer C.M. Pennington Richards would tap into that Nesbit-ian aspect of life-as-paralysis, one which veritably rules, albeit in different guises, in our modern technocratic world where the displaced self, depression, fear of one's very identity, and the over-reliance on the bed—and the becalming oblivion of sleep—reign like the elfin beings in Dickens' own proto-*A Christmas Carol*, 1836's "The Story of the Goblins Who Stole a Sexton." Those impish—but daemonic—creatures actually take a man down into the earth, just as we so now readily tend to take ourselves away from true human connection, spiriting away our innate natures in exchange for whatever pose we deem most crowd-pleasing.

Dickens wrote *A Christmas Carol* while walking upwards of twenty miles in the English night of the fall of 1843. He was betting on himself, his career having hit a trough on the commercial front, which meant that *Carol* would be self-published, and with a blinding turnaround at that. We generally think of Halloween as the haunting season, but Dickens—and the gang behind 1951's *Scrooge*—knew all together better about the real scariest time of the year, and tapped into the power of that knowledge.

The autumn depends upon the sun for its grandeur. We need to see the spangling of colors, of the gourds, the pumpkins, the leaves that visually parallel our perpetually advancing mortality. That pigmentation provides coloristic fuel to the tales of specter and charnel house stirrings. Washington Irving wrote "The Legend of Sleepy Hollow" (1819) as a brand of ersatz, evanescent Englishman, far from his New York home of the Hudson River Valley, but Ichabod Crane's ordeal on that Hessian-defended bridge means less if the prismatic shadings of the fall are not present and refulgent in the reader's mind. You almost have to be caught up in the foliage. The scenery. An amount of light. This is a world surcharged with exteriority. Seasonally dependent. Weather dependent. A natural world, which, if we read the text to the end, has a natural explanation. Jealousy, a prank, comeuppance.

The sun beats a retreat as Christmas draws nigh, vacating its place in the sky well before five o'clock, which is what I think of as the time when the ghosts come on, as Dickens surely did, too. Most of the day will be dark, which seems ideal for haunting, and also plumbing the mysteries of that which haunts us.

Some will do so willingly, others will recoil, pull up the jacket collar and say that "all is well," as if mere repetition powers a fait accompli, a version of "ignore the problem and it will go away."

Other people need to be enjoined, lent some help, prodded, pushed by a friend who is able to do so with carefully chosen words that are sufficiently skilled in their bedside manner that we'll allow them to get through to us. Sim's Scrooge is so brilliant in part because though this inducement is necessary, and requires the services of a most multi-factorial member of the undead in Michal Hordern's Jacob Marley, we also have this tinge of belief that he wishes to make his Orphic journey, but is terrified at his inability to get himself started. He fears his failings. They lock him in place. And how many of us can fail to relate?

So there I am, not long before Christmas, in the library nook, beholding stills from *Nosferatu* (1922) and *Bride of Frankenstein* (1935), wondering if I will ever be able to see these actual movies, or if that is impossible now, and you had to have been from many,

many years before—what lucky dogs!—and down two sisters, fearing that my time for familial effacement will be coming as well, sans warning.

I had a grandmother who called me a bastard—which is what I technically was—and we'd have to go over her house, something I hated. My aim was to skulk off when we were there, hide myself in the plain view of the living room not currently being used. As a meal was consumed in the kitchen, I took an apple or some such covertly into this room, where the TV had been left on, the dance of its flickering images and lighting effects accentuated by the encroaching crepuscular shadows outside.

It was on one such afternoon that I descried Edward Van Sloane as Van Helsing in the Tod Browning 1931 version of *Dracula*. I hadn't seen the start of the movie—there was only this curious, bespectacled man who I just knew had some huge piece of information that was about to rock a bunch of worlds.

He was holding a kind of grim court at the bottom center of the screen in an operating arena at a teaching hospital, commenting on two puncture marks—made by you know who—in the neck of some fair English lass, now quite dead and covered in sheets that gave off a heavy cerements vibe, not unlike the haunted linen of our man M.R. James's "Oh, Whistle, and I'll Come to You, My Lad" (1904) (a recording of which will be made by none other than Michael Hordern in the years following his brilliant, story-transforming turn as Jacob Marley in *Scrooge*).

The rest of the world, and that house, the people in it, ceased to be relevant for me, even extant. There was only that moment of the beholding, the cognizance that here was acute fear because also in that moment I lacked the requisite verbiage of description. Sensation, feeling, was total, as if the body portion of Descartes' famous dyad had a hegemony that now ruled my mind and rendered it both mute and moot.

Later I might have likened this moment of lacuna in my life—a sort of between the acts interlude—as akin to a first orgasm which comes accidentally, when one does not know, truly, what an orgasm is. I was changed. I didn't know how, but I knew that I was.

The reason that *Dracula* aired that late afternoon was on account of a program called *Creature Double Feature*, a staple in Boston at the time, which utilized the old Shock Horror package of vintage scare-fest movies that were provided to TV stations in the late

1950s. You didn't go to the actual theater to see *Creature from the Black Lagoon* (1954), if your parents even would have let you. You caught them on the sly, in the interstices of human existence, your human existence, which is also how we will see Michael Hordern as Jacob Marley approach Alastair Sim as Scrooge at the culmination of an otherwise quotidian day that is all the more galvanic—and Galvanism will mean even more to Scrooge than the famous creation sequence of James Whale's 1931 *Frankenstein*— because of the context of its unfurling and what I will call a psychical detonation and a piercing of the veil of self. The otherwise voided self. The buried alive self.

The television set resides within home and hearth. It already has ingress in your innermost outer world, if that makes sense, the place in which the guard is let down, where we care less about how the world might perceive us. We're in the dingy sweatpants, the ripped T-shirt, where we are generally most comfortable with ourselves. The sanctuary. The place of respite, where we recharge.

But there is a potentially dangerous dichotomy—we may too often retreat to the home. Sometimes we all but have to force ourselves to leave it. We engage in behaviors deleterious to our health that we would not engage in—or to the same degree— elsewhere. The home is such a conjoining with who we are, that people who wish to end their lives will often repair to a hotel instead, so as not to be pulled back, calmed, stilled, encouraged to carry on, by the familiar.

Home cuts many ways at once, as I certainly knew from a young age. And as Sim's Scrooge also knew from his own beginnings, shipped off to a private school, seldom returning even for the Christmas holidays, on account of having a father who would have preferred to blot him from the official family record, in stark contrast to his sister, with the sibling aspect obviously standing out to young me. That's a level of fundamental abnegation that can only dovetail with the darkest of horror, though perhaps we need a more Poe-esque phraseology—let us say, then, raventail, with the darkest of horror.

When Sim as Scrooge returns to his rooms on Christmas Eve—rooms once belonging to his now-dead (sort of) partner Jacob Marley, he feels put upon. There had been Cratchit to deal with throughout the day, with his Yuletide zealotry; those nettlesome collectors for the poor; the admittedly prepossessing, but distressing, Nephew Fred, with his role in having ended the life of the one person Scrooge believed had cared about him; even that mendicant-ish man who buttonholes Scrooge outside of the stock trading exchange and begs for additional time to repay a loan. Scrooge craves his sanctuary—even if it does look like a haunted house of the Edwardian era—and his repose. But an infiltration is at hand. An intervening hand from out of the shadows, from out of the earth, the past, the recesses of psyche.

The year my sisters were removed from our home, and I was, after a fashion, de-siblinged, my mother made sure that I had a greater trove of Christmas presents than I knew what to do with. You would have said it was a spoiling, and she would have termed it a worthwhile one, after what I thought I had lost, but which really she had lost more than anyone, with my father cast in the role of stoic rock which sea and wind buffet, but neither erode.

I still wasn't sure, though. My guard remained up and locked around me, a force field of protection. Toys, I considered, were effective in making that guard come down, could be a parent's way of tricking you. I was loved, but the home was a place of terror.

There may come a point in one's journey of fear that one chooses to conduct experiments on that fear itself, a gathering of information. Robert Frost—who certainly knew something of the encroaching darkness of New England nights, both in the literal and figurative senses—wrote that "the only way out is through." He's speaking of an embrace of horror. The surcease of running. The jettisoning of trying to explain away—that is, rationalize—and the business of acceptance, which is a process.

Over the years of watching *Scrooge*—a picture I've seen more times than I'd be comfortable guessing—I have increasingly been struck by the haunted man's complicity in putting his soul on a kind of terror blast. Often with terror there is a component of the rapine—psychological rapine, but rapine all the same. To what extreme must a human go to to essentially say, "I lay myself down, I resist no longer, end me or help me to be me again"?

Dante comes to the gates of hell and is told, via a placard, to dispense with the quality that is most crucial—hope—to human existence. To arising the next day. To continuing on. It's not money, stability, friends, family, even love, for one can be unloved and alone, and yet still possess hope that one will not always be so. When hope goes, so too does the last penumbraic flicker of the candle. All that remains is darkness. The darkness we find during the Christmas season, when the ghosts that haunt us best, say, "Now's the time, boys." The pooling darkness of the chestal cavity where the heart all but asks, "Wait? What has happened here?" as out goes the light.

Dante sees the placard, and on he continues. Is there a braver, ballsier decision in all of art? His direction is downwards, more overtly damnable, whereas Sim's Scrooge goes airborne, hand touching the robes of his ghosts, which are different—and they know this, of course—than *his* ghosts, which can be much like the ghosts that make a Bogeyland of our lives all of these years later.

Sundered as a man and close to giving up the ghost of hope, the English poet, John Clare, found and mined a stunning pocket of resolve in his 1848 poem, "I Am," written five years after the publication of Dickens' *A Christmas Carol*.

Clare had been dubbed the "Peasant Poet," and had a brief dalliance with fame a quarter of a century earlier, when he was feted in London. Around this time, Dickens was about the same age I was when I discovered the definitive movie version of his story of visitations, a horror film that gave me a better understanding of not only what horror was, but what could be done with it, what we might call horror's higher purpose, if we've correctly valued ourselves.

The early Clare wrote of the countryside with an enlivening eye that had a knack for enduing robust nature with even more robust nature, the gift of an elemental animation such that one would think the trees possess the required energy to dance, if only they wished to use it. In "I Am," we find Clare much transformed, poeticizing in terms to resonate with anyone who has journeyed across their own version of the nightmare vistas that Brian Desmond Hurst would bring to life in a mid-century movie:[1]

> I am—yet what I am none cares or knows;
> My friends forsake me like a memory lost;
> I am the self-consumer of my woes—
> They rise and vanish in oblivious host,
> Like shadows in love's frenzied stifled throes
> And yet I am, and live—like vapours tossed

As we'll see, this three-stanza poem could double as the official verse of Sim's Scrooge, a character with roots in Dickens, but one whose footfalls dot the interior spaces of all of us; that rare character who is in one manner rooted, in another sui generis, and in a third malleable to whatever our own personal experiences—and demons—may be. A trifecta unlike any I am aware of in cinema.

In the early sequences of Hurst's picture, the viewer encounters Scrooge on his own, walking, eating, brooding. The mind, in solitude, is rarely the tabula rasa; rather, a highly personalized variant of ink all but drips from its pages, an accession of words that we can't help but read and reread (one reason, conceivably, why it can be so hard to be on one's own). It's not difficult to imagine sentiments like those expressed by John Clare passing through the mind of Sim's Scrooge, in what is tantamount to his downtime—an oxymoron if there ever was one, when regret and self-doubt carry, and haunt, the day.

My own inchoate sensibilities as a horror-loving boy, with his comingled fears of the known and the unknown, a mixture of family history and a kind of ocean-drying, internal wind of self-doubt that I lacked that which was necessary for love and belonging, could have done with a dollop of John Clare, not that I had his verse at hand. But as we'll also see in our exploration of *Scrooge*, hands themselves—actual, physical hands—have a knack for reaching from the screen and beckoning us. Touching and guiding us. Toward a bed. A grave. Our prior experiences and choices. Tasks and challenges of better-built futures.

We are dealing in the transformation of the previously oblivious host—and, of course, Clare is punning on the idea of transubstantiation, just as Hurst will—into an actuated being who is a living, breathing, skin-clad, human spirit—and an inspirited creature—without the weighted appurtenances of a Jacob Marley, who is the after-the-fact friend with his beseeching reminder to fully inhabit the while-you-have-it life. The less one does so, the greater one's personal terror quotient, which a viewing of *Scrooge* will caution us is not the pleasing variant of M.R. James's Yule digressions. We're talking a Christmas horror that extends through all the parts of the calendar and a life, a horror that plays for keeps.

Never underestimate stairs in horror cinema. They are symbols that connect worlds, and which mark a passage from one into another. In *Scrooge*, where baroque balustrades repeatedly pack a doozy of a wallop, it is a staircase straight out of German Expression—upon which one would not be surprised to witness a quick cameo from *Nosferatu*'s Max Schreck—that brings us to a kind of paradoxical, overland netherworld, though the street of the city is but twenty feet below.

A man has come home. He expects the comfort of familiarity, an evening of no new developments, even if he isn't entirely sure that he didn't just see the face—in the form of an agonized death-rictus—of his late, perfunctory friend and partner, who probably wasn't really his friend in life as both men looked at the world.

Sim's Scrooge journeyed up to his bedchamber, whereas I, a child, an only child as Scrooge himself had come to be, departed my bedroom, unable to see the time on my *Star Wars* (1977) clock where C-3PO and R2-D2 tolled the bells, and made my way, late one evening near Christmas, in that year after my sisters had been taken away, downstairs to the room where my parents would watch TV.

I heard the set playing, which must have meant that at least my father was there, being something of a nighthawk. But there was no other living form in the room when I got there, at least not as I understood living forms at the time. But there was a movie playing on the old RCA unit that had not been switched off, and in this movie a man was sitting in a giant bedroom, so large that I thought at first that it was his entire home.

The man had soup, but he was not eating the soup, for there were bells that were ringing. So many damn bells. The man screamed, unable to endure the sound of relentless, ringing bursts of brass staccato. When he screamed, the sound stopped. The man waited for something to happen, as he seemed to know it would, even had an inkling what might be coming, though already I could tell that nothing like this had ever happened to this man. He readied himself for his visitor, our Mr. Scrooge, this self-consumer of his own woes, who still lived, who still was, as per the lines of Clare, but who did not live well, and who already knew a terror that would dovetail—raventail—with the horror newly arrived upon the scene.

When you are seven, eight years-old, you do not say to yourself, "I have skin in this game," though from our earliest dabbling with cognition, we feel when that game is afoot, and our skin is on the line. More than skin. Skin is but the door, the covering, the ripped-aside coating. I did not yet know that this was Alastair Sim, and that airing in the dead of the suburban Boston night, on a station that carried Bruins hockey games, was a film belonging entirely to its own category, and a horror picture of more consequential depth than any whose stills I sat agog over at the local library, pleased that the sun had probably gone down outside, and that my mother had not come to fetch me yet. But skin I knew I had, and so I sat down on the baize carpet and watched, and Jacob Marley, carrying enough chains to enwrap a houseboat and pull it to the bottom of the sea, made his way up to Scrooge, and made his way up to me.

FOOTNOTES

1. The Clare poem is easily located. I'm partial to the volume *I Am: The Selected Poetry of John Clare* (2003), from Farrah, Straus and Giroux, but www.poetryfoundation.org will also take you where you need to go.

Reel II: Curse of the Stand-Alone Miser

Personal connection is perhaps the most efficacious route into what a film, or any work of art, offers us, but some films are better at providing the substrate—or the aperture, if one prefers—for the facilitating of that connection. They make it easier for us to come to them, and vice versa, because of what they say about who we are, either at some earlier time in our lives, or in that precise moment, the *nowness* that produces a concomitant sensation of, "It's as though this was made just for me."

The greater the number of people who can feel that simultaneously and independently of each other, the greater the legs a work has to roam, reach, impact. And to inform our lives years, decades, centuries, millennia after their creation, a concept that, as we shall see, can more properly be called "re-creation."

When I intimated to some people that I'd be writing this book, exploring the horror components of a movie with an easy—and misleadingly overriding—Christmas connotation, their responses were similar. There was evidence of an abiding affection—a love—espoused in the hearty and hale tones of a Nephew Fred for this particular picture. It went without saying—to those who had experienced it and drank deeply from what is ultimately, I'd maintain, its loving cup—that it was the definitive take on *A Christmas Carol*, which has had no shortage of cinematic treatments, to understate matters. We're talking a veritable filmic Yule log in Dickens' original source material—a Yule log that never burns away and works just as well the next year. The 1951 *Scrooge* was what the cognoscenti preferred, just as Beatles enthusiasts know that you need the English versions of their albums, not American mash-ups like *Meet the Beatles*, and admirers of Buster Keaton would sooner pitch their home video sets into the harbor than watch the colorized version of *The General* (1926).

Every generation seems to have at least one kick at the Dickens Christmas can, going back to the age when members of the public viewed motion pictures as a brand of sorcery, enabled by the technological strivings of an Edison. Cool stuff for a story that was always, centrally, a work of ghosts, whether the ghosts reached their audience via parchment form, the shadow plays of the camera obscura, or imprinted on celluloid.

But I think viewers regard 1951's *Scrooge* as the go-to choice and the various other interpretations as relative pretenders—claimants for a throne that does not belong to them—precisely because it is so *real*. Psychologically real. These undertakings are the best offerings of terror art, where supernatural horror is human horror, and by that I don't mean it's the ghost of some murdered woodsman who's come back for vengeance. Rather, the fear comes home to roost in something we perceive—or apperceive—about ourselves. The difference in those modes of perception is that the former can call upon us to deal with something we prefer to set aside at our current station in life, and the latter can throw the past into focus in a manner suggesting that forces we had assumed were dead, wished were dead, tried to ignore into being dead, may pull our future apart and render us a decedent who just happens to have blood flowing in the veins—a mere technicality, after a certain point.

We are cognizant of the supernatural, but even when the supernatural has been isolated, we're left knowing that it was but the messenger, an intermediary of fear, in the service of the real horror which is not the making of malingering, post-human entities. It's often us. It's often that which has been done to us, or that which we think has been done. And our response. Our wallowing. Or the will with which we adapt and pitch ourselves back into the fray, or don't.

Henry James understood this component of "us," with *The Turn of the Screw* (1898), and Shirley Jackson in *The Haunting of Hill House* (1959), and it's an all-but-official thesis statement of Brian Desmond Hurst's film, a dark miracle of the picture in that it takes no qualitative artistic backseat to the book that helped make it, before it made of itself, I'd suggest, an autonomous work of art. Yes, *Scrooge* doesn't exist without *A Christmas Carol*. But I've never watched the film and thought that it wasn't separate from what Dickens scratched out with his pencil, if you follow my meaning.

In America, there was the far-rosier 1938 version of *A Christmas Carol*, a comparative tinsel strip of lightness and whimsy directed by Edwin L. Marin with Reginald Owen as the hard-bitten skinflint who becomes an after-the-ordeal avuncular stalwart and financier—somebody had to pay for those doctor bills—of the previously doomed and now preserved Tiny Tim. The turkey juices were scarcely dry on granddad's whiskers after Thanksgiving dinner, before the Owen version of *A Christmas Carol* took to the airwaves in the States, all plummy and pleasing, for those preferring—needing?—the roseate over the real.

Horror films breed and stoke passion and loyalty in a way that few other films do. The term "cult film" has come to suggest artistic failings, with a degree of winsomeness and charm nonetheless, but don't be misled—"cult" just as often speaks to the avidity a work of art inspires. Doesn't mean low numbers, necessarily. Rather, it's indicative of a nature of a bond. Horror films are the pictures most often tagged with the cult label, because we unionize to their cause, after a fashion; we have symbiosis, shared purpose. We belong to a group, but said belonging required no forfeiting of individuality—rather, it celebrates it. And that is why we come together. The sort of picture that might be tapped for an Oscar, as a contrasting example, trends to the genteel and banal, with no such binding element as horror provides. You don't stop and stay—you dabble, say, "Oh, okay, this is what's going on here," and move on. You probably remember next to nothing about the picture after you've sat through it, because that's just what people do with those kinds of movies.

So it went for the Reginald Owen airing of the Dickens tale. Any horror was sanitized, as if those oh-so-cute Cratchits could afford a maid and she had scrubbed it all out. There'd be no charnel house, no picking over the belongings of the dead, and the ghosts have a greater concern for conviviality than scaring the living shit out of somebody in part to remind them that were still alive.

In 1938's *A Christmas Carol*, Owen's Scrooge—who is more irked than disbelieving, like the neighborhood kids have pissed him off again—actually calls the cops on Marley. The constables come into the room, see nothing—Marley merely takes a load off out of view—and tease Scrooge for being a drunk (cue bad pun about "spirits") and depart, leaving Marley to pop back out again and essentially say, "See? I told you I was real. Can we get down to business now?"

By calling the film *Scrooge*, director Henry Edwards and screenwriter Harry Fowler Mear were trying to differentiate their effort from those that had come before in silent form, and the ubiquitous novella itself. A new wrinkle.

Other variants on *A Christmas Carol* have poured out some horror, but the aperitif version, not the full flagon. From 1935, there was another *Scrooge*, with Seymour Hicks as the master of parsimony, looking far more aged even than his sixty-five years. This is the first sound version, and perhaps over-excited about the advent of this new-fangled technology, the movie rather over-eggs the pudding—or maybe just stinted on the budget—by having Jacob Marley appear only in voice form, courtesy of Claude Rains, who had already taken a voice-driven star-turn in James Whale's 1933 Universal horror, *The Invisible Man*, a film sharing the mordant wit of our *Scrooge*.

That early sound version of the *Carol* mangles the Jacob Marley-visitation opportunity, which is what it is: a chance to take the movie in a direction that will make it more than some holiday affair, yet another nugatory chestnut-roasting-on-an-open-fire that just happens to be the movie theater screen.

The horror of 1935's *Scrooge* stems from its roughhewn, folk art quality, a *mise-en-scène* suggesting that if you'd turned a rock over in nature, this movie might have crawled out, festooned with bits of pine needles from years ago: crinkled, frowsy, hirsute, a fringe of snakeskin for a hat. You could even say that it looks like a movie that was made before movies were made, a ghost of an entity that never had a chance to die, but a ghost all the same.

1970 produced another *Scrooge* with the Albert Finney musical slant on the penny-pincher's redemption, and again we see the surname-as-title used as differentiator. The scares of the Finney film arise from the juxtaposition of the grim and the musical; you walk through a cemetery late at night, and it's probably scarier if the person you're about to come upon is singing a tune than happening hastily along his way, which would be disturbing enough.

A 1984 made-for-television version of *A Christmas Carol* starring George C. Scott and directed by Clive Donner was an attempt to get very serious indeed about this nasty Scrooge bloke and what was wrong with him. Donner had the track record and the firsthand experience—he served as editor on 1951's *Scrooge*, invaluable to the look and rhythm of the film. The colors are washed out, Scott looks old, the movie itself all but groans like it has a seasonal cold in the lungs and its sciatica is acting up again. Realism negates magic, rather than bolsters it. Overwhelms and supersedes it. You think, "Sad.

Downer." Not, "Scary. Holy shit," with all that those last two words can imply—on earth, and not on earth.

Sim and Hordern returned twenty-years after appearing in *Scrooge* to reprise their roles in a 1971 animated short given the title of *A Christmas Carol* that was theoretically for children, which scarcely any child has any business watching, lest they—and their parents—are copacetic with a few years of nightmares. This duo clearly understood—their performances, riffing on the 1951 picture, bear it out—the power of foregrounding fear when it came to the seizing, empathetic nature of the story, as they had helped to twist it two decades prior. Fear buttonholed the viewer. "Took" the viewer, just as the viewer would later take what they had experienced in that film out into the world.

The best horror films—and likewise horror-driven literature, music, paintings, even radio plays—impel us to all but tap the breast as if to say, "I get it in here, the realest way," sharing that ardor and knowledge with other members of a de facto club who appreciate the multitude of levels on which we may be frightened.

Fig. 1: The Scrooge-ian visage.

Monsters with root causes are always more frightening than supernatural interlopers that have no more to do with us than where we happen to live or the graveyard we've wandered into. I think this accounts for the loyalty that comes from those who spend a lot of time (if you've watched 1951's *Scrooge* once, I'll bet my own proverbial bottom dollar that you've watched it a dozen times) with Hurst's *Scrooge*, their devotion and certainty that the movie cannot be topped as an interpretation of *A Christmas Carol*. But

I also believe there is something that occurs on what I'll call lower levels of the brain, beneath our surface thoughts and feelings, in mists that account for the psychological and emotional forms of the spiritual epoxy that most bind us to a work of art.

Having professed undying allegiance to their love of *Scrooge*, these various people with whom I spoke would often pause, ostensibly grappling with an epiphany while I waited, mid-conversation, and add, "You know, I never thought of it as a horror film, but it has always scared the bejeesus out of me."

I'd think, "How could it not be a horror film?" *Scrooge* is many things. It's different than any other interpretation of the Dickens work—and part of me is uncomfortable classifying it as an interpretation, when it's so much more—and arguably any other effort in cinema, because its motoric drive comes in part from its singular amalgamation.

It's a seasonal work (albeit one that in both tone and the larger implications of the plot is not confined to a single season). An effort of hardcore realism that prefigures the British Kitchen Sink movement which will arrive at the end of the decade. It's an art picture, utilizing the deep focus photography we experience in the cinema of F.W. Murnau and Orson Welles. It's film noir, with the high-contrast white/dark light and shadows of 1940s American crime/thriller pictures in thrall to documenting the bad choices made by anti-heroes coming undone while the rest of the world sleeps. We have multi-generational family drama. A mortality play laced with gallows humor to make an undertaker blush—though not the hell-seasoned, impish undertaker of this particular film in Ernest Thesiger.

Ah, but those ghosts. There are the four official past masters on that score in Jacob Marley and the triumvirate of spirits of which he speaks, but then we have the ghosts behind the ghosts, as I think of them, and these are the ghosts that can all but devour the ghosts we see for breakfast, as if ectoplasm could pass for cereal.

A man who is completely alone, friendless, believing himself to be beyond the age when any change is possible, riding out a sort of death-in-life string, is indeed ripe and ready as a horror character, *is* horror, in a way. The walking, horror incarnate.

When you are an individual whose very existence might invoke the question, "Would death be worse or better?" then the horror element is at full play. If the future cannot be advanced upon in a manner where growth has a theoretical chance of occurring, because the past has come to own all, then you have terror. Anguish. A patch of living hell in the form of the freeze-framed life, and the knowledge, on some level—and it's worse when it is not that most topical one—that here you sit and here you will stay. Self-flayed, in one regard, but unable to do anything about it. Or so it feels.

The horror is complex. It possesses gradations. Rather than existing as a single color, it's the ROYGBIV terror spectrum, and when we have a spectrum, we can be less focused on the single label, an individual coloration. But consider the spectrum in full, and we really lock down on the intensity of the overarching concept.

Readers of M.R. James will be familiar with what his fans now often call the "Jamesian wallop"—that moment in his fiction when the horror of the canvas—his page—surges forward in a torrent of undried impasto, with a stabbing motion.[2] There's a shadow-clad, obscuring leap from the uneasy, tenuous foreground and out into the world that can feel like a body blow to the reader.

Brian Desmond Hurst and company make of the wallop something more bestial, but psychologically so—the body, the heart, the soul, is worked over from first to near the end. Not the last, because a horror film needs release at some point for maximum efficiency, because what the best horror films do is set up a series of contrasts where what *is* plays off of what *might have been*. Scrooge will give us the ultimate release at its close, and one well-earned, because in the release and euphoria, our associations, the memories we have just had made for us, will return, Proust-style, to the life that "had been" with pre-transformation Scrooge, a life we desperately could not handle our own lives resembling. And yet—

It's that "and yet" that kills you. Questions that we entertain, our doubts about what we're doing, how we're living—if we really are locked in on that digital age cliché of "my best life"—float surface-ward with Scrooge.

Every person who has ever sat down to a watch a film is a selfish viewer. It's not a bad thing. It's human. We look to see where we fit in. Even with escapism for reputed escapism's sake. We think a character is somewhat akin to us, and in our viewer's eye we go to them. As a child, that's whom you're going to dress up as, think of yourself as, sans the garb, on the playground. The adult leaves the costuming aside—well, there is Comic-Con and Halloween—but that Kino-Eye that Dziga Vertov understood so well in his 1924 film of the same name, a movie ultimately about how we perceive and apperceive, is imperishable. And we all have it.

Scrooge is a horror film that it goes beyond the accepted trappings of the horror film. It's like how no one says about Babe Ruth, "Well, he was a good ballplayer." A ballplayer, yes, but the term is extraneously diffracting—it spills and separates too much meaning.

But what I will call the creation scene in *Scrooge* wastes not a drop of dread. Not the haunted man variant. Not the variant of the past times owning one's present day mental health. Not the ghost variant with the twist that the ghost in question has come into a job that is part essential, part unfulfillable, a kind of mind fuck for all eternity. (There is much method to the madness of this picture's unique insistence on putting Jacob Marley in a more central role than in any other adaptation.)

The scene I walked in upon as a young boy—catching, as it were, two giant eyefuls of extreme horror *in delicto*—is a grimoire tour-de-force writ in the most devilish, and paradoxically loving, forms of what Alfred Hitchcock called pure cinema, but which I'll posit as a cinema both of, below (as stylized hell-scape), and beyond this earth. It's supernally human. Otherworldly in its worldliness.

Alastair Sim's Ebenezer Scrooge has just settled in for a long winter's night. He is already cognizant—again, on some level—of the long winter's night that now doubles as his stalled, embalmed life, one that is a life because death is yet to be technically accurate as a descriptor of his biological station and status. He has no idea how long this night will eventually prove. He's an accursed guy in his own mind, with the entire world feeling as if to conspire against him, but he does not know what he does not know. He's about to start to in the following scene of horror that is matchless, because every effect of lighting, editing, performance, sound, script, coalesces into a single question: How have you really been living?

As we'll glean in our exploration, *Scrooge* induces terror across that aforementioned wide spectrum, but it won't get you, or me, any more than it does in that moment when you feel that you have to answer—if only in your own breast—the query it poses to you when the ghost form of Jacob Marley has come and gone from the ghost—with the human-coloring—of Ebenezer Scrooge, and perhaps your own ghost form as well.

As I said, we all watch movies selfishly, which is different than being selfish. Then again, so is existing from living. That is the very knife's edge of horror, and we go the way we go. A fight for life, a need for life, has many forms. Outlasting Jason and his hockey mask in a barn is but a single type, having that silver bullet handy for the Wolf Man is another.

Knowing, or fearing, that one is dead inside and the lone possessor of this knowledge, is the terror that dares not even name itself, or rarely does, which is buttoned down, hidden away, growing, festering, feeding, consuming mind, soul, heart, and coming often enough, too, for the body, which feels like comparatively lower-stakes.

And yes, of course that's horror. What on earth, or not on earth, could it otherwise be?

FOOTNOTES

2. M.R. James inspires quite the fandom, and what that fandom does is get to talking. At first, I was taken aback by the level of devotion. There are any of a number of places you might find his work voraciously discussed on the web – Facebook groups and the like, where I do considerable lurking. I do want to recognize the chummy, typically riveting A Podcast to the Curious. These James fans have their familiar terms, and one of them is the "Jamesian wallop," which you'll hear various times on A Podcast to the Curious, and note elsewhere. James buffs use it as a form of shorthand for a staple of the author's best tales. But that aside, you're going to want to check out A Podcast to the Curious. They cover every single work James published—and some he didn't—and works by authors he influenced or loved. Can't recommend it enough. You'll have a blast.

Reel III: Tickled Bleak

Inscribing a copy of his 1934 novel *Tender is the Night*—its title sourced from a line in John Keats' ghostly "Ode to a Nightingale"—F. Scott Fitzgerald produced words to the effect that if their reader liked *The Great Gatsby*, they'd be knocked headlong by the new effort. *Gatsby* was a tour-de-force, he maintained, but *Tender is the Night* was a confession of faith.

I have thought often about that distinction—and how the two ideas might blend, and do blend—in each instance when I watch Jacob Marley pay his ghostly visitation to Scrooge in our 1951 film. For it is a tour de force of horror filmmaking, and a confession of faith—a heraldic divulgence—in the power of terror art and terror cinema. In the power of its very moment and act of unfurling. And in a willingness to attest, to insist, that, "look, we know you think you're getting a Christmas film, all cheek and charm and redemption, but that is not the business of today."

Keats composed his sonnet in 1819, roughly two and a half decades before Dickens night-birthed the novella with terror elements that later doubled as springboard for the ultimate in terror cinema.

Keats was near the end of his life. He had ramped up his pace of composition as if knowing that his earthly time is winding down like a watch that can never be reset. Haunts—the revenants of lost and doomed love, missed opportunities, self-designed ghosts—fills his verse. The stanzas are replete with what we may think of as emotional fetches: those doubles for ourselves, in less-than-human form, ghostly variants of those who are not dead in the corporeal manner of death, but have their separate spirit form nonetheless.

Tender is the Night is similarly haunted, and likewise *Scrooge*, a point which is hard to deny after the visitation scene, which is also a form of creation scene. Efficacious horror may start on the outside. We experience it in the world. 1962's *Carnival of Souls* is chock full of images to drive its protagonist, Mary Henry, back into the watery grave from which she's had temporary respite, but the horror makes its greatest inroads on a different plane, that of the internal schema. The world within the self. It is the knowledge of dread, that something may be true, which one does not wish to be true, that acts as a kind of root of the horror chord, or a home key.

The reason that Lucille Fletcher's 1941 radio play, "The Hitch-Hiker"—written especially for Orson Welles to perform—works as well as it does is because as the young man travels across the country, running into the same, lonely figure that seems to outpace him despite having no car of his own, there's a subtle elision of the horror of the external into a horror of the internal.

A shift occurs. That shift is powered by culpability, or presumed culpability, with there being a great chance the ascribed culpability is right on target. We have levels of knowledge in our heads. The top level is as basic as, "I think I will have a ham and cheese sandwich for lunch today, I haven't had that in a while." But there is another, more influential level, which maximizes fear, because we regularly seek to avoid what this level is telling us, and we can become adroit at keeping it from the surface, where the business of today's lunch is worked out. But the level is dominant. What goes on there, voice-wise, is akin to a chorus shouting at us and shaming us, and it may seem as if new voices are added each day to the point, the argument, the thesis, it is trying to impress upon us.

We may loathe this level, in part because we struggle with locating the courage and problem-solving tools to turn it from a voice we are aware of in the pit of our being, to one nakedly out in the open, where we can deal with that voice. "Solve" it, as though it were a math problem. This is the level that stalks and hunts us with its truth. It's the level of haunting, the level of terror, and it can be such that there is not a ghost or monster on earth to touch it.

Fletcher cribbed part of the idea for her nightmare of the radio from E.F. Benson's 1906 short story, "The Bus-Conductor." Benson had been one of the members of the Chit-Chat Club, those horror lovers who gathered in the Cambridge rooms of M.R. James at Christmas to experience the annual fictional wickedness their beloved antiquarian had produced. These are post-Dickens artists using Dickensian tools of folklore and tales of the holiday-gone-wrong, but with *Scrooge*, we're not mucking about in a stylistic laboratory limning Victorian themes of repressed feelings and too much damn curiosity for one's own good, which is James's specialty.

We are dealing in the max external, and the max internal, a full powering-up of two kinds of horror that appear to be separate, because one emerges with sufficient violence—an assault of our senses—that it commandeers all of our focus. This is what takes care of that top, conscious level of thought. We are locked in. And as we are locked in, the thoughts below—the doubts we have—see and seize their opportunity to make a push into our conscious minds. It's a very fast turnaround in a movie like *Scrooge* from, "Wait, what the hell just happened here?" to "What just happened to me?" Consider it a more entertainment-based version of the turnaround that comes with shock and trauma.

Think about the times you fell out of bed as a child. Your mind immediately starts trying to determine what has occurred, where are you, why do you hurt, why is a hard surface below you, even as you cry, and call out for mom and dad. You have shock and sensory overload, unfamiliarity born of sudden, violent newness. You've experienced a kind of body blow, and you are hyper-focused even in your confusion on the attempt to understand the physical sensations and how they came to be.

But the real fear—which is explored during the early stages of this deductive process—is that you've lost your stable center. You may feel as if you've been attacked, but you know not by what or by whom; that someone has done something to you they shouldn't, though you also feel as though you are alone, and you are "the doing," as you may be again. How can this stop? Is this to be how it now is?

Mom and dad enter the room, the light is turned on, hugs given, and someone lies with you for five minutes until you drift off again. But a worry, a fear, has situated itself inside of you, and it resides on that level where the choric voices share with us what they have to share, as we try to focus elsewhere.

As Sim's Scrooge makes his way to his rooms—which, in this film, had previously been occupied by Jacob Marley, and are the rooms we see him die in via a flashback later—he experiences the lower-level haunting of the self out of the corner of his senses, we might say. An emotional peripheral vision that follows the onset of raised hackles.

The ghosts of the self are not easily dragged into light, aren't caught full view, unless we mount supreme courage. Scrooge takes these ghosts—the ghosts of Scrooge himself, the living man who is also a form of dead man—and gives them external form. In the lead-up to what we'll call the big reveal—when Michael Hordern's Jacob Marley all but jars apart the bones of Scrooge and us, too, the viewers, with his official advent—Scrooge stairs at the knocker of his house, unsure if it really just morphed into the face of his dead business partner and nearest approximation to a friend.

The Dickens novella—and every other treatment there has been of this source work—makes no pretense of a friendship between these two men. There is the puling line Scrooge offers to Marley's ghost—when he thinks that the ghost might toss him a crumb of mercy and perhaps only haunt him with two upcoming ghosts rather than the full gauntlet of three—about how the two had been buddies, but it's not sincerely felt. We don't believe it, and nor does Marley.

It's a line of a person speaking a certain way because they want something and someone else might give them what they want, Scrooge not yet understanding the relationship between Ignorance and Want like he will later in the film when the Ghost of Christmas Present opens his robe and reveals his terrible, beastly loins, with their warped fruit in the form of bedraggled, raw, terrified children—as if, Macbeth-style, they'd been untimely ripped from a womb, years after the fact, rather than too early. The unclean, unwashed, primal, living ghosts of the Id-voice, the inner stalker of conscience, which is another possible name—at times—for the lower-level choric voice that makes no luncheon orders, and pursues us instead, until we come clean.

What is coming clean? It's not necessarily fixing an issue, or at least not immediately. It's putting the issue on the top level, examining it, and working on "what now?"

The 1951 film is the only work derived from the source that shows us what passes for a friendship. And also why the friendship itself is haunted, and why it does not work because it is based in disconnection; that is, the nature of the false friendship is enabled by two individuals precisely because they each become more disconnected from themselves. Theirs is a union of trumpery. Of name only. When we persist in anything that is in name only, which ought to have actual value, the choric voice never lets us forget, even if we do not tacitly acknowledge what is happening. Sim as Scrooge sees that doorknocker, which he tries to write off in his head as a mere reflection, or the blurred vision that comes with fatigue. He had a long day. Cratchit was annoying.

Nephew Fred unrelentingly cheerful, that fop, etc. And so, into the house he goes.

Until this point in the film, we've had a day in the life—with Christmas trappings—of Ebenezer Scrooge. The weather of London itself seems haunted, a free-for-all of shadows and blanketing snow that appears as a death shroud of the city. The face of the metropolis has been covered.

Fig. 2: The dark night of the soul/teeth of inclement weather.

Coming out of the trading exchange where Scrooge does the portion of his business that we figure he enjoys the most—as if it's his football pitch, where he beats back the dreams of other men—he's accosted by a man to whom he's lent money. The weather makes the duo seem as if they're part of a shadow play, and what we're watching isn't quite real, though certainly it's a very real horror for the fellow who begs for more time to repay his loan. Sim opens his mouth, and right away we notice those teeth like ablated fence slats, human and not human at once. Scrooge rebuffs this man, who appears to melt into the ground, defeated.

We have such a fuzzy sense of time. You watch the beginning of the film transpire, and you think what a netherworld this is. It's how we'd expect a world to look at three in the morning, not somewhat near the close of the business day. An unnatural order prevails upon what is the natural way of city life. The year comes to an end, the days become shorter, but C.M. Pennington-Richards' cinematography already enchants—and worries—us with a darkness that glows. This ought to be a contradiction in terms. But we see a similar effect achieved in the shadow boxes of Joseph Cornell, or Barnett

Newman's 1949 luminously obsidian canvas, *Abraham*. The latter redefines how one might view the color black, which is a dominant background shade. Think of the night's sky. The stars are in it, but don't you always think of the stars as the foreground, and the sky as the background? But it could be the other way around, right? Or they could be on an equal planar field footing. Cornell, Newman, Pennington-Richards all repurpose the color black as a foreground tool. The color becomes the conductor of the visual orchestra. Black is active in *Scrooge*, not passive; it waves the baton.

The film noir aspect is pronounced. When we watch a film noir from this period—and we're smack dab in the meaty part of the chronological noir curve—we're conscious of wet nighttime streets. They glow, they have shine without over-brightness. They pull us in.

That is the function of the snow in these early outdoors scenes, but they also provide a spectral quality. The whiteness of the snow seems to emphasize the darkness of everything else. We're anything but at ease. We may even feel cold, as if the film itself—this early mood—is leeching into us. This is the way a crime picture is lit and shot, with the tools of horror. The wind does not stop like it would in most movies, so that we can better hear the dialogue, which you'll notice happens often when the camera cuts to a tighter two-shot. The man who has button-holed Scrooge is only twenty quid in the hole, but there will be no mercy for him—in fact, Scrooge almost begins to laugh when the poor guy cites the time of the year, the season of generosity, forbearance. He receives a shove for his troubles, a raw hint of violence, the beast within.

When Scrooge sets off towards his counting house, where Mervyn Johns' Bob Cratchit awaits, he plunges further into darkness. The city is a wilderness that swallows him up, but the imperious nature of his stride asserts his lack of concern, as if via leg-based boast and taunt. He's a man who is either not frightened, or trying to convince himself that he is not. Another Christmas, and he's alone.

Seven years previously, Jacob Marley died. The evening marks the anniversary of the parting of Scrooge and Marley, the death day. The outside wall of the counting house is itself lambent, with, again, that idea of glowing darkness, what we might experience in William Hope Hodgson's *The House on the Borderland* (1908), a druggy, dream state of a novel where architecture exists between worlds, and relationships are caught between worlds as well. The known and the safe are replaced by the subsuming and the deadly as the protagonist is ferried away from his home, to other dimensional planes. The prevailing disorientating state is akin to the child who has fallen out of bed, before it realizes what has happened, but stretched to the length of a cosmic horror tale, which is where Scrooge's life has been trending long before we see him this night in his own borderland as he returns to his counting house.

We're feeling the cold, we've identified with the man who has pleaded his case for the loan extension, thus dialing in on the rude physical contact Scrooge makes with him, but we're still not prepared for his behavior as he walks down the street of his business. Children are caroling outside of the counting house, having reached the middle of a rendition of "Silent Night." There's scarcely a carol that is so charged with reverence for a good greater than ourselves. Up comes Scrooge, and shoves the kids out of the way.

Fig. 3: Seasonal noir and thwarted carolers.

I grew up in an era when there was spanking, and it was considered discipline, even if my parents never brought hand to bottom. But I recall how much this shocked me the first time I saw the scene, when I was less scared of Scrooge—ironically—than I was *for* him.

He is the portrait of a lost man, established as such in these two efficacious scenes that encapsulate his brutality and "lost-ness" from the human race. That non-stop wind would fit well in Algernon Blackwood's "The Willows" (1907), with its rustling leitmotif of the damned. These city scenes are elemental. There's a quality of raw nature in them that our "Peasant Poet" of the woodlands, John Clare, would have appreciated, perhaps known to be leery of. We're not on a soundstage, but in the actual streets of London, kitted out as Brian Desmond Hurst saw fit. The snow has sheen, but it's also dirty snow, the kind you know not to play with, and a snow choked with the grime of a sooty metropolis. It is the soot that rots lungs, and it curtails mortality.

From the begrimed snow alone we have a foreboding for what the poor parts of the city must be like, the slums and the hovels erected in alleys, the gaseous fog of the rampant factory age descending upon all. Sim's Scrooge doesn't break stride—he walks right into those children, shattering the moment of peace, innocence, purity. A man doesn't do that out of mere villainy—he has darker, intensely personal reasons, and they typically come from a past that haunts him.

I knew how the plot played out, when I first began watching *Scrooge*. But this was the moment when I understood—with certainty—that the story would not proceed as it had elsewhere. All might come right in the end, but the progression wouldn't be the whimsical, faintly spooky course that the novella took, nor certainly the sugary stroll of the Reginald Owens 1938 picture. No satire here—which I think was one of Dickens' aims—and no 1930s piffle.

I both wanted to see what would happen to this man, and didn't wish to see it at all. Not out of indifference, but rather concern. That the price would prove too high, to use another phrase from F. Scott Fitzgerald, which he meant in the context of what the making of that art had cost him in his life. For Sim's Scrooge, I wondered if the price was too high for him to see what needed to be seen, for this person to reverse a course. If truth and reality would crush him, and maybe it was too late. The baseball Hall of Fame catcher Yogi Berra had a saying: "It gets late awful early out there." When does it get too late for any of us?

The day that appears like it has always been night rolls on. We're versed in the exchanges at the counting house and how the byplay will go down, if we've seen any production of *A Christmas Carol*. Two alms collectors come 'round asking for donations. Nephew Fred arrives, robustly played by Brian Worth. He's my all-time favorite Fred, and let's remember that few characters in all of art are more purely likeable than this one. I see horror in the look of beseeching sadness with which Sim's Scrooge looks upon his nephew. It's the sadness of wisdom, and I don't believe it exists without self-knowledge.

Scrooge knows how far off the grid of humanity he is. And in that look—which is pitiable, and all the more remarkably so, because we just watched this guy shove a child—we know that he knows what he is.

Writer Noel Langley takes liberties with his Dickens the way Orson Welles would with Shakespeare. In the novella, Fanny Scrooge—Fred's mother—is Scrooge's younger sister, but Langley has made Scrooge the younger sibling in this film. Fanny dies giving life to Fred, which rips Scrooge in half—he wants to detest the young man, but in him he sees his sister, who had a maternal presence in his life, filling a void in large part because their own mother had also died in giving life to Scrooge.

The two men are linked in death, but they do not carry that death the same way, because Fred surges with energy. We know that this energy flows into every aspect of his life. Fred is a "can do" guy, whereas, Scrooge has ceased to live in this manner long ago, and has lost two mothers after a fashion. Love of a past memory—that for his sister—puts a damper on his hate, which is the animating force of his life. A twisted life force, certainly, but all that he has. Or thinks he has.

Sim's eyes are like snow globes as he looks upon Nephew Fred. I think, "If ever eyes could hold a person, the way that arms do, it would be these eyes." They want to reach, and they cannot reach. They indicate a desire to bridge a gap, but there is no surmounting that lacuna-space of this particular borderland in which Scrooge is in the world, and out of it. That is to say, he has entered into ghostly form. He's a fetch.

Soon we will see actual limbs—or former living limbs, if one prefers—that also seek to reach and cannot. The details and the associations of Scrooge stack in ways that our conscious mind might only note them after a dozen viewings, when we finally "get" why we've both been surprised by what we see, but also readied for it out of the corner of our eyes, our senses, by our own choric voices.

The humor in the Dickens novella is provided by the narrator, with little originating elsewhere. The narrator is impish, who or whatever he is. Maybe it's a ghost-scribe, The Ghost of the Book You Are Holding. Certainly, Scrooge is himself rarely this master of wit within Dickens' prose. Cratchit endeavors to get by, not have his kid die, knock back a few Christmas ales. Humor is not in his ken. Fred is bonhomious, but serves forth no comic lines. He strikes me as someone who likes a good joke more than he's apt to tell one. The first two ghosts have their moments of rascality, but they are not laugh-inducers.

But humor is crucial to *Scrooge*, because of what humor means for tragedy, and how tragedy can send us rocketing past the edge of terror. I am not sure there is anything more frightening than post-terror, when terror has just broken you. As a concept. As a way of life. Post-terror is post-caring and post-feeling. It's why Herman Melville's Bartelby freaks out everyone so much, and all but drives his employer mad trying to help him—to help him help himself. Post-terror occurs when we are post-self. We've left the station of our own lives. And where are we going? I don't know—nowhere. The Borderland. To take up residence inside a Cornell shadow box. To wander like chain-attired Jacob Marley. Only, we have to go to work on Monday morning.

The first act of this film builds to a climatic scene that is also a starting scene. Hurst has Scrooge in motion. The idea of a journey is subtly instilled. We're so accustomed to theatrical productions that *A Christmas Carol* can seem sedentary, stagnant, all but happening around a dinner table. In place rather than in flux. But Sim's Scrooge flows from the start, even before he takes to the sky, shooting across blackened seas under cover of blackest night.

Hurst employs cuts so that we first see Scrooge walking in one direction, then coming from the other, in his approach to his counting house. For all we know, he ventured fifty yards, but we feel as if the journey has been one of length—he's walking hither, he's walking yon. The lost soul in the business of wandering. The alley that he emerges from before disturbing the caroling children is a form of a declivity, a cutting, similar to the railway cutting of Dickens' short story, "The Signal-Man" (1866). Again, duality—he's above ground, but we view him as below ground. A prelude to the grave. Subterranean repose. Which, as we learn from Jacob Marley, is not quite how it works.

When Scrooge closes shop for the night, we see his one moment of cruelty in the film that smacks of being planned, a conscious attempt to hurt, and not a reaction to someone around him—the man in the street asking for an extension to repay his loan, the caroling girl. And it is nasty. When he rebuffs the alms collectors, he's not cruel. He is a jerk to the loan guy, but he also spends time offering counterpoint. He has his reasons.

Now, those reasons don't speak to a generosity of spirit or a willingness to do more than is legally necessary—pay taxes, for example, or give the landlord his rent check—for one's fellow man, but he is amused by the back-and-forth with the alms collectors, anyway. To him, he's sparring with these guys. You know that person who loves to argue for the sake of arguing? Scrooge has that quality, in part because he has nothing else, so far as person-to-person contact goes. We could even say he's a pre-internet troll.

Mervyn Johns, meanwhile, is an owlish Cratchit. He's not nebbish. He's not meek. He's in a bad position with no leverage. British horror fans knew Johns as the similarly owlish architect of 1945's portmanteau *Dead of Night*, the character whose haunted dream provides the framing story, fusing the individual movements of the film together. (The film, incidentally, includes a version of the aforementioned E.F. Benson story, "The Bus-Conductor.") *Scrooge* is also a frame-film, though not historically classified as one. You could watch parts in isolation and they hold up as stand-alone shorter pieces. And we are coming to one piece that could function as a self-contained highpoint of horror if there was nothing on either side of it—though let's be grateful that there is.

Cratchit lets slip a final "Merry Christmas" to Scrooge, and my goodness, that beat—the pause of gathering rancor—by Sim. He holds this beat before answering, and the raging disdain that spreads across his face is a look of death.

The disdain cannot be entirely for Cratchit. He doesn't inspire it. We already know that for Scrooge, personal familiarity breeds maximum contempt. "Peace" comes when he is having at others, with that sparring that he probably needs to have in order to feel any overlap with the world at large. This is a man, in Scrooge, who might as well be looking at himself in a mirror and wanting to kill.

"You a clerk on five shillings a week," Scrooge says.

He doesn't even need to add a dismissive shake his head. It's such a dehumanizing passage, a self-dehumanizing passage, concluded by, "I'll retire to Bedlam"—shades of Val Lewton and Boris Karloff and their 1945 RKO picture of the same name. Horror buffs could even mistake it for a shout out from Langley to the earlier film, though it isn't. There's humor—Scrooge is having a joke—but it's so in tune with the graveyard that we're experiencing the humor of post-laughter. Edgar Allan Poe had comic sensibility of this variety, and likewise Ambrose "Bitter" Bierce, for whom, I think "An Occurrence at Owl Creek Bridge" (1890), with its famous ending of the soldier, who thinks himself spared, instead having his neck snapped above a river, was a form of ghoulish hilarity. Sim is not gaunt, but he has an ability to look cadaverous. Reanimated. Mackenzie Crook, as Gareth Keenan in Ricky Gervais and Stephen Merchant's *The Office* (2001-2003) shares that characteristic. Keenan is a toady; he's a right-hand man, which is what I guess Cratchit is for Scrooge, but also an emaciated vampire. He sucks the life out of fun, of people trying to connect with each other and grow their relationships. He's what was once called a "buzz kill." Sim's Scrooge is similar, and his countenance works in the same fashion. We want to study their faces in their singularity; with Scrooge, we're visually drawn to what repels us because of what it represents in this moment of emotional barbarism. This is a buzz kill type of fellow on a monstrous level.

He's saying this demeaning line to Cratchit to amuse himself, a form of a "Now that was a witty jape by me" move. He'll replay it in his head. Of that we are certain, and the humor acquires the coloration—a paradoxically bloodless coloration—of the tragic. But he will replay it in his head because he's alone, and thus has to supply all of the fuel of his own internal conversations. At least he has his intelligence, he thinks. After all, other people don't.

To me that's horror. I've been that alone in my life that I've read the email I sent to someone ten times. I didn't have anything else. Anyone else. One enters a state of Ouroboros—the serpent with its own tail in its mouth.

Cratchit doesn't possess Scrooge's intellect, though Johns elevates him above the level of dullard, or meager bean counter, which is essentially his occupation. He's elated to leave and see his family, drink his porter, but we watch as Scrooge picks up on Cratchit's tact, his pity. Though insulted and reduced, Cratchit does not wish to insult and reduce in return. We've watched Scrooge do nothing decent thus far. But he earns what is tantamount to sympathy in the horror medium. He's that lost. He's that lost to himself. The kicker is that he's not fiendish. He's not a bigger bastard than people we know, leaving aside the bit where he smashed into the children. We've all known the look from Cratchit that Scrooge receives. We wonder when we last received it, what it was that had caused us to lose the path of our own lives. Maybe even lose ourselves. We've probably all given someone that look, too.

Scrooge has a final stop before heading home for the holiday. He's at his nadir. Ironically, terror will serve to rally him, tease out his humor so that he's in on a joke, rather than a joke himself, a person whom one gossips about. We see that early on, with his fellow money lenders at the exchange, who literally laugh at Scrooge when he tells them his plan for the evening, which does not include any attempts at making merry.

His coiled scarf is wrapped over his mouth, and as he approaches the hostelry where he'll take his meager dinner, there's a visual gag—and a visual pun. A man with a sign around his neck saying that he is blind, with a dog and a stick, flees as Scrooge approaches, noiselessly. Composer Noel Langley has supplied him with a contrabassoon theme. We'll often hear it as a series of legato notes, but in this sequence it's an extended cadenza. Even the blind man can see what Scrooge is. As they say: Boom, roasted.

The more frightened Scrooge becomes—when the source of the fright has an external aspect—the more alive we see him as, so long as he figures the terror comes from outside of himself. In the company of an official ghost, he bears up. Adrenaline does not fail him. Perhaps he would have been a huge horror film fan, half a dozen decades later. But it is when he is on his own, or confronting an element of his constitution, that Scrooge is the haunted man incarnate, and Sim makes him look over-guarded to the degree that a mouse coming out of an unexpected hole could give him a heart attack.

He has this meal, and he requests extra bread—presuming it's free. Told that additional bread is extra, the response is immediate: "No more bread." Sim delivers the line like it's the vocal version of a guillotine coming down and lopping off a head. Swoosh. Plunk.

Sim taught elocution, and boy does he land full-stop on the end of words, sticking the verbal landing. That flourish provides his language with an angularity matching his features. The line produces legit guffaws in the audience. I've never watched this movie with anyone who didn't laugh at this juncture, with the request for more bread and then the reversing of the request. We need humor to bolster the tragic, and tragedy does humor a good turn, too. They contrast. They're foils. They are not allies in intention, or results, but they are allies in bringing out their respective depths.

There will be lots of doom in the next passage of this film, but it wouldn't come—nor be so potent as it is—without the contrast, or by serving gloom after gloom. We've had a funny moment. It's at Scrooge's expense, and the staff at the inn that serves him his meal will probably have a laugh about Mr. Scrooge as they clean up and head home to their families for their own merry-making and stock-stuffing. The humor warms us a trifle—the shot of whisky in the frigid night. We'll need it.

Consider Scrooge's appearance here: in the restaurant, he wears his gloves, without their finger tops, to eat. Who does that? He's hunched in on himself, like some crab. He doesn't just break off an end of the bread—he rips it like it's something living that might bite him if he doesn't ablate with alacrity. There is an expression of disappointment clouding his face upon passing on the second helping. A gaze of "so it has come even to this." Composer Noel Langley's theme for Scrooge, a half dozen legato notes of contrabassoon, pipes in, a rumbling in the pits of our stomachs. A man chews bread in a pub. But at this point the movie is absolutely saturated with dread. A Last Supper for one.

But hark—I hear the first strike of the carillon, and, wait, what is that? Ah, the beating of your heart, as you doubtless now hear mine, and we need not even stand within the space of each other's elbow.

The time has come, as an unholy, atonal carol of the bells is about to play in a chamber of rest, sleep, that is also a wood-paneled mausoleum of death, the animate decedent on display, and in his pajamas, no less, with the winter's cap that you read about, as they say.

So: silence the scrape of your own chains as you shift and get cozy in your chair, for we would not wish to encroach upon the ghost of Jacob Marley's big moment, and let us steal our way forwards, enter this room, and behold a scene that is the very cinematic definition—and rendering—of human horror.

REEL IV: HOUSE OF SCROOGE

We've seen Scrooge's day in the life, the man going about his business, which we experience as a recounting of the norm—his norm. In the Beatles' 1967 *Sgt. Pepper*-closing song, "A Day in the Life," the devil is in the mundane details. A man reads a newspaper about a death. He smokes (smokes what?) and falls asleep on a bus. Those quotidian scraps of info harbor a sense of dread, though, and they build to cacophonic, atonal release. They escalate to death the way life does. Or is it that they build to rebirth the way that life can? As we see, accept, grow. But within both the song, and *Scrooge*, through this portion of the movie, we're swept from the garden variety day, with its admitted notes of ill-portent, to what is essentially a gale of nightmare. We might not see it coming, but when it does, we feel as if we should have.

Another winter walk, from the restaurant to the rooms where Scrooge lives. There are no other residents as he advances towards us, no revelers straggling home, no caroling children. The camera is positioned with a full view of the lane to the left, the door to the right. The snow is cleaner than the precipitate that we saw with the first outside scene on the steps of the trading exchange. We know there is less traffic in this area. The well-heeled live here. A quoined wall in the background looks like a furrowed brow, tilted off its angle. There's depth to this shot, and all of it is in sharp enough focus to make Gregg Toland proud. I don't think there's a film that looks crisper than *Scrooge*. You can see every last hair, every puckering of skin, the last link in an extended ghostly chain.

Until this scene, Hurst has used a number of medium shots. Now he's pulling back, opening matters up, taking a top off a box, allowing us the wider vista. Scrooge has actually been walking for a while before we can detect him, despite our vantage point. There's a shadow along a fence, and it conceals his true form entirely until he steps clear of it. The effect is jarring. We're unsettled, unsure how he crept up on us like that.

The notes of the contrabassoon melody are spaced further apart as Scrooge arrives at his door, and the camera moves in tight to him with the felicity of an F.W. Murnau shot. A wash of cymbals, but dubbed low in the sound mix, and then the voice of Michal Hordern, as the ghost of Jacob Marley, that voice pitched in the exact same register as the contrabassoon. Thus, Scrooge and his dead partner are auditorily linked.

The door knocker has the face of a lion. Scrooge bends down to retrieve his key, and when he looks up, he sees the visage—in ghost form—of Marley superimposed over the knocker. The face is in anguish. Hurst cuts to Scrooge for a reaction shot, and his own countenance matches Marley's. The two men—or entities—have this beat of recognition, where eyes meet and appear to gesture to each other in shared cognizance.

You won't get this in other adaptations. Most directors think it's enough to feature a form dissolve and show Marley's mug in place of the knocker, a cheap scare out of Disney's Haunted Mansion ride. There is no communion, which is what happens here. The feeling is not a comfortable one for any of us. Scrooge appears as if he's beheld a killing or act of pederasty—there's total disgust on his face over what he has seen. His mouth hangs open, those fence slat teeth in full view, the scarf—which I think of as Scrooge's version of a security blanket—now dropped down.

"Jacob Marley?" Scrooge asks, the words extending in dilatory fashion, unlike the rapid fire "No more bread" line we'd experienced mere minutes prior, in real time. The ghost visage melts back into the brass knocker, Scrooge twitches twice—like a person who has been touched upon orgasmic release, the flesh remaining sensitive—and opens his door.

Fig. 4: German Expressionist stairs in Victorian London.

The camera is waiting for us on the other side, so that we see Scrooge from the front, at the base of the baronial stairs, an inversion of Dwight Frye's first glimpse as Renfield of Dracula—"I bid you welcome"—in Tod Browning's 1931 Universal picture. Scrooge casts a look behind him. Maybe he is checking to see if some pranksters had a sort of light box and threw a spooky shadow, or he's uncertain that Marley, in one form or other, could be nipping at his heel. The stairs, the staircase spindles, a gate, throw a spider web of shadows, pure German Expressionism. To enter this house is to become encased. You could seamlessly splice this composition into *Nosferatu*, or a Jacques Tourneur film noir, the tendril textures of *Stranger on the Third Floor* (1940), or one of the early cod-supernatural haunted house pictures like *The Cat and the Canary* (1939) or *The Laurel-Hardy Murder Case* (1930) so prevalent between 1920 and 1940.

Those American films of that era had less-than-supernatural explanations in their final reel, a tradition that would linger with Browning's 1935 film, *Mark of the Vampire*, itself a remake of a "See? There's a perfectly logical explanation after all" film, Browning's 1927 Lon Chaney vehicle, *London After Midnight*. Those films aimed to comfort and appease viewers with the pacifying idea that the horror would be rinsed away in the end, and the horror itself was induced by the sets, the lighting, the ratcheting up of tension. Pragmatism prevailed.

But I always felt like the viewer was being let down from their tenterhooks. Protected. So it went, too, with filmic adaptations of *A Christmas Carol*—you didn't get horror because of glad tidings and all, a brand of cinematic well-wishing. I think that Brian Desmond Hurst would have considered this a disservice to the public. Scrooge himself is not owed his haunting, but he is aided by it. The more real, the better. So, too, does it go for us, the viewers of *Scrooge*.

Scrooge comes to his own house seeking shelter, not unlike the stranded travelers in James Whale's 1932 picture, *The Old Dark House*. Whale liked his wit, and Hurst likes his, too. Black humor enlivens terror; it's not a depreciator. The home in the Whale picture always feels like some mud-encrusted hut that is just barely keeping out the entirety of the rain, despite the otherwise airless Gothic design. We sit by a fire, but we're conscious of the dripping water collected in the bucket a few paces away. Scrooge seeks his shelter on a dry night. The air is crisp, the snow packed, echoing the footfalls. But Scrooge might as well as have just been drenched by a nor'easter at sea, so heavily does his environment appear to register upon his face. Now the shadows will enfold him, and lock him in their grip.

Scrooge has made these shadows. As Dickens' narrator tells us—and tells us wonderfully well in the 1938 radio play of *A Christmas Carol* with Orson Welles doing the narrating—Scrooge loved the dark, because the dark was cheap. He enters spaces he chooses to keep as lightless as possible, because Scrooge himself is shadow—human shadow.

We've seen him move undetected in the radiant snow. Now he comes to burrow further into his world, as so many of us do, until he has to leave it again. We take to the room, the screen, the Netflix account, the phone, wrap up into a ball, sequester ourselves away, take on our shadow form, nix the identity, lose the identity.

In the parlance of our day, we might say that Scrooge is settling in for a staycation. But that won't recharge his batteries. Plus, a house guest is en route. It's not a guest that is coming to dinner as in the 1939 Moss Hart and George S. Kaufman play, but it will put in a post-prandial appearance; and, in the realest way, that guest will never leave. Its host will have to absorb him.

***

I've always found graveyard ghosts and their ilk among the least scary of apparitions—the stuff of Scooby-Doo. When we view a setting as ripe for scares, it's inherently safer because we've recalibrated expectations. These are the ghosts too "on the nose," as I regard them.

Both E.F. Benson and M.R. James understood the shock value of a ghost in an incongruous setting. With "O, Whistle, and I'll Come to You My Lad"—a story that our Michael Hordern will record a reading of, and also star in a 1968 BBC television adaptation—James creates peerless horror by having the ghost—which may be an avenging demon in quasi-human form—pursue Professor Parkins on the beach, during the afternoon, advancing over the groynes as if they were not there.

Similarly, in what most James aficionados rate as another of his best stories, "A Warning to the Curious" (1925), poor, crown-excavating Paxton is dispatched in grisly fashion alongside the seashore on a beautiful spring morning. We think, "Wait, what is the horror doing here?" and that is the finest horror, because it's the horror most like life, which does not wait for a given time to let loose its latest fresh hell upon us.

Destruction for Jonathan Harker seems avoidable in Bram Stoker's 1897 novel *Dracula*, until one otherwise benign moment, when he comes upon the Count making up his bed, having no staff in the castle, which is when Harker understands that everything is way, way wrong, and there could be no leaving this place. Yet this simple act of domesticity, the Count fluffing Harker's pillow, will make your blood gelid.

As we travel deeper into Scrooge's house—by mounting the stairs—we see how suggestive it is of the haunted abode. His living rooms are Gothic, with their high ceilings, the implication of a draft we all but feel as we watch. The manner in which Scrooge ascends the stairs —after having locked the door, checked and re-checked the lock— suggests a sexton with a lantern making his rounds. Dickens' *A Christmas Carol* had a piecemeal dry run as a sketch-story embedded in The Pickwick Papers called "The Story of the Goblins Who Stole a Sexton," in which a Scrooge-type is carted off to the underworld, just as Scrooge will later fly over Victorian London and the very mists of time themselves. A sexton is a lonely job. If the pay were better, it's not a stretch to imagine Sim's Scrooge putting in a resume and applying for the post. What is about to occur in this house would then be transitioned to the great outdoors—or the city graveyard slant on them. Then again, Scrooge lives in what's tantamount to an indoors cemetery.

Stairs are underrated in horror. They mark a traversal from one plane to another. They're readymade symbols. The vampire in *Nosferatu* is never more unnerving than when we see his silhouette advancing up a staircase. Eleanor Vance, in Robert Wise's 1963 film, *The Haunting*, is told, in ghostly chalk adjacent to a staircase, that she must remain within Hill House. When another noir-esque film, 1947's *It's a Wonderful Life*, segues into terror mode, it does so on a staircase, when Jimmy Stewart's George Bailey decides that now is the time to take his life, for which he leaves home and hearth behind to do just that, scarring his children, I'm sure, for the duration of their own lives, never mind the happy, tear-jerking ending.

Scrooge comes to a dead halt at the top of the stairs, as he once more hears Marley intone his name. John Williams must have made a note of Richard Addinsell's score as Scrooge reaches this standstill, because it's a perfect ringer for the *Jaws* refrain. A minimum of notes, a maxing-out of effect/impact. Scrooge looks meek—a child who cannot handle the dark. He rebels against that meekness by trying to snap himself once more into his prevailing character, slashing at the air with his hand, declaiming a rather stutter-y "humbug." Then he's once again in flight, but with this tantrum mixed in.

Today we'd make a flippant remark about Scrooge's principle living room being his "man cave." The walls are dirty. We can see dust upon them, marks from fingers. Scrooge does not clean. At the same time, we feel the cold air, which prevents the room from taking on a dowdy sensation. Senses are on high alert in cold rooms. Scrooge sneers as he closes the door above the stairs—a victory sneer. He's eluded…what? Capture? Having to see a ghost? Damnation? Whatever it may be, safety is achieved, or so he hopes. He hangs up his scarf—his warming security blanket against the world—and says another "Humbug," elongating the syllables this time, because his confidence is on the uptick.

Clearly this is a comfort space. Scrooge has dined, and now he will have a post-meal/pre-bed soup, which he retrieves from the hob. I identify with Scrooge here. He's enjoying his small treat. In a limited, lonely life, you look forward to meager procurements—the slice of pizza at the bakery after a long, grinding day at work, with no one waiting for you at home. What he does not know is that a bedeviled symphony of wasted life is about to begin. Consider this the moment at the concert hall when the hallway lights flicker, alerting you that now is the time to take your seat, for the orchestra is about to tune up, and everyone to be on their collective way.

The camera dollies towards the chair where Scrooge sits, stirring his broth. The motif of the contrabassoon—reminiscent of advancing danger in Sergei Prokofiev's 1936 symphonic poem, *Peter and the Wolf*—has us in its euphonic hold, both pleasing and warning at once. Scrooge appears vulnerable as we look at him from above—not near the ceiling, but a few feet over his bald pate. Just as he is to take and savor his first spoonful of what I think we can assume is cheapjack slumgullion, Marley says Scrooge's name again. The soup dribbles back into its bowl.

This is the theater of tension that earmarks lasting horror. The lead-up. Exordium. When we cannot bear something *not* happening. We desire to get it over with. No matter how awful it may be.

Clang goes the spoon in the metal bowl, a subtle effect, but one which will pay off. The rattling is a prelude for the bells that are about to go off. The sound of struck metal has been gently pressed into our minds, a kind of "Wait for it, wait for it…" The tinkling of chimes commences. They are angelic at first, festal. The expression on Scrooge's face, though, is one of panic. He knows for whom these bells are tolling.

As a wandering child of the night, during the Christmas season, in a house where I felt both at home and also not where I ought to be—which is how I figure Scrooge feels here, because that is how he feels to varying degrees in even the most hospitable of places—this is where I entered, sat down on the shag carpet, entranced. Continuing with the theme of duality, I was frightened and not frightened; the former for obvious reasons—this is taut, intense, scary stuff—and the latter given how every frame of this particular sequence impels a viewer deeper into the movie.

We'd spoken of that concluding crescendo of the Beatles' "A Day in the Life." The sound is initially low, easeful, but it gains in pace, volume, soon becomes a controlled caterwaul. Director Brian Desmond Hurst has thus far inserted silences—the way in which a composer uses rests—so that they are integral to the mounting of tension. That first tinkling is the contrast—a shock of the new, and the interloper. The interloper is not a physical being—and he won't be. But he does have a brassy, daemonic fanfare as entrance music.

The initial tinkling is akin to a cantus firmus, a work polyphonic in nature with one of those musical lines then being fed into a larger, fugato structure. That's exactly what happens now with the sound design. I don't know this for certain—no one does—but Hurst must surely have worked closely with Addinsell on what happens next. Bells go off from all over, as if an unseen giant is playing a gargantuan-sized carillon. The melodic lines are complex, interwoven in ways that would have roused J.S. Bach. Later the rock band Pink Floyd will lift this construction wholesale on their 1973 album, *Dark Side of the Moon*, with its track "Time." The song features its own opening movement of bells, oriented in what a 16th century composer like Josquin des Prez would have known as a paraphrase mass. The Pink Floyd song is about running out of precious time in one's life, on account of wasted moments—the unlived life. The life of existence. The Scrooge-ian plane.

The warped caroling of the bells builds to demented pitch, the sound coming from all angles of the room, out of every darkened corner, under every dusty rug. The clocks, too, rebel against their metronomic nature. This isn't just Shakespeare's unnatural order, it's an explosion of time itself. Even the small hand bell on Scrooge's side, where he ordinarily sets his bowl or mug, turns against him and joins the fracas of brass gone mad.

Editor Clive Donner cuts between that diminutive bell, a grandfather clock, chimes above a door, in a fashion similar to the cutting between faces, the heavens, Boris Karloff's arm, and Colin Clive's manic gaze in 1931's *Frankenstein*, the film that put James Whale on the horror map, with a huge assist in that scene, which is a masterclass of editing, courtesy of Clarence Kolster.

Hurst used that earlier film as a roadmap for this essential scene, upon which so much of his film rests, and will use as a fulcrum, in the way that Orson Welles studied the set-ups of John Ford's *Stagecoach* (1939) for how he wanted to make *Citizen Kane* (1941). In both *Frankenstein* and *Scrooge*, the respective fulcrum scenes are creation scenes, reanimation scenes, birth scenes.

With the Whale picture, Karloff's Monster—"It's alive! It's alive!"—comes to life, after a fashion. With *Scrooge*, the stunted miser—and that's really the least of his problems as a human—embodied by Alastair Sim has obtained a chance—though he doesn't know it yet—to come to life. For both scenes, terror is the driver, for different reasons. Henry Frankenstein has gone too far. "Now I know what it feels like to be God!" he shouts, as the blasphemous celebrant, while a disapproving clap of thunder resounds overhead. Scrooge, meanwhile, is ready to soil himself.

There's a reason why so many people know Boris Karloff's Monster as Frankenstein. When you're a kid, and someone asks you who you're going to be for Halloween, prompting your response of "Frankenstein, duh," there's no one who thinks you're dressing as a mad scientist. You'll have the green greasepaint, the gash in the forehead, the electrodes. Frankenstein the man and the Monster become fused; especially in Mary Shelley's novel, their lives, minds, natures, run on parallel tracks, until they intersect. The beings blur.

We can assume—and later parts of this Brian Desmond Hurst film bolster our assumptions—that many people mistook Scrooge for Marley and Marley for Scrooge. When they strike up what we'll call their friendship—though it's a friendship between two frightened asps who prefer to attack before being attacked—they do so because of their commonalities. Each recognizes in the other what has come to define himself. Empirical, witness-able documentation of their original relationship isn't present in the Dickens novella. Scriptwriter Noel Langley provided the duo's backstory for this film alone.

We've not watched that backstory play out as of yet, but this scene utilizes the power of rapprochement and rapport that is to come. The twining of these two men. 1935's *Scrooge* went with that title choice as a differentiator, to provide a new wrinkle. *A Christmas Carol* as a name-brand was already deep in the culture and the tradition of the Christmas holiday that Dickens himself had helped give its modern meaning. But that's not why the 1951 masterwork goes by the name of the human scourge that Alastair Sim will go a long way towards turning into a human of purpose, who transcends the errors of his ways, pastes over the cracks in his personage, and de-monsters himself.

Other adaptations posit Bob Cratchit as the Everyman figure, but not the Hurst film. Sim-in-the-character-of-Scrooge is the foundation of relatability on which this film mounts its ideas, imparts its lessons, and does so most often through terror. We've been looking at how Hurst has humanized Scrooge at the start of the film, how his team has worked to present a thesis declaration of sorts that this man isn't that different than us. His monstrous quality is not that of villainy. Other Scrooges have the Darth Vader aspect. Big bad meanie. But not this one. He's a living—as in breathing, money-earning, loan-granting—decedent. He's what one used to be able to call a member of the walking dead, before people thought you were referencing a TV show.

These bells, in this creation/visitation/birth scene, toll for him, surely. But they just as surely toll for us—or many of us, anyway. And I find that to be one big, deep, graveyard pit of horror, because it's just so damn…everyday-ish. The devil is in the details, which makes it harder for us to cite him as what he is, explain what he's doing. A murder, yes, sure, we get it; that's a splashy talking point. But the specifics that go into daily life? The thousand little "tells?" That's the horror that can take our voice away—itself a horror—because it's a struggle and a battle to tell people what we think we know, either about ourselves or about others. Those details are blown up into larger form—after all, this is a movie. Then again, we can also say that here's a guy having an issue with the clock in his house. What is more theoretically mundane—banal—than that?

But these are not quandaries of life that Alastair Sim's Scrooge is pondering in the short pause when, like the roiling crescendo of "A Day in the Life," the roar of sound halts, as if some grim conductor of the witching hours has called off the dogs. There is a moment of silence. Another well-placed rest. Within this liminal space, we find what I maintain is the apogee of terror in cinema, not that we'll spend the rest of our time sniffing roses in Kensington Gardens. Far from it. Scrooge is the Everyman. Scrooge is us. And he is stone cold terrified. He knows the reckoning is at hand. He knows it is a self-reckoning.

The door flies open and we get the final note of this movement of the symphony: Scrooge screams. All is forgiven if you do, too.

Reel V: Them Scrooge Eyes

I had a friend once who maintained that you could tell if someone was smart or obtuse by how they looked. The theory sounds garish, even offensive, on the surface. Pressing her on the subject, she continued, "There's a way people can be observed in engaging the world. Passively or actively."

I'd ride the subway, playing a game of testing my friend's theory, watching rider upon rider with glazed over eyes, such that you might think you could have waved a hand in front of their faces and produced nary a blink.

The eyes are a big part of what my friend meant with her argument. The rare rider had eyes that darted, but not manically. Rather, those eyes scanned a car for clues as to what gave the space its notable points of meaning, interesting objects, other compelling faces, what information might be gleaned in an unusual advert. These eyes searched, and they also pulled a world into them. Light-beam eyes, and absorbent eyes. You even see it with the eyes of some babies—they drink in what they experience through an ocular capacity, the active witness, never as the creature of passivity, even before they can produce an understandable word.

These are the eyes of Alastair Sim. They are part of what makes him perfect for the role of hoary skinflint. The shock of white hair, the reflective pate, the high-set cheeks, like fleshy vales, eroded by time—or through having rubbed them in despair—all serve to frame the eyes as if foregrounded in a nightscape that has taken the form of a man. With the face of Alastair Sim, everything returns to the eyes.

In *Scrooge*, he communicates with them, acts with them, registers knowledge, issues warnings to keep away, pleads for mercy, and eventually bestows kindness on others with those eyes. The teeth of which we have spoken give Sim a quintessential British look. They're not bad teeth, rotting from the skull. They're not misshapen, but they are large, resembling dentures without being dentures—I don't think George Washington's famous chompers could touch these teeth for character—and they're certainly idiosyncratic. I nurse my own pet theory that some of the best character actors are English and Scottish on account of the propensity of those countries for producing arresting faces. They are quirky faces our own observant eyes lock onto, and, more importantly, faces that impart some of the person within.

Alastair Sim, born October 9, 1900, in Edinburgh—and who would die in London in late summer 1976 (five years after his second turn as Ebenezer Scrooge in the animated version of *A Christmas Carol*)—was an unlikely choice for Scrooge, but luckily we have Brian Desmond Hurst and his ingenious casting against type to thank. Then again, much about Sim and his career had long been unlikely.

Professionally speaking—though he took a while to find his calling—Sim's job was viewed as making audiences laugh. He was droll, with the unteachable gift of timing, a hint of Bob Newhart to him before Bob Newhart was Bob Newhart. Sim excelled at wit, and certainly wasn't a pratfall man. There was nothing broad about his sharp, precise humor. He may not have made everyone laugh at a theatrical production or in one of his films, but those that he made laugh, laughed long and hard, laughing in the way such that when it's a fortnight later, a well-delivered, on-the-button line is remembered, and one chokes on the breakfast tea.

Prior to his thespian career launching at the age of thirty, he also worked as a laborer and a clerk in a government office. Apparently, he wasn't the easiest fellow with whom to get along, but the qualities that made him difficult to know at times also had their admirable components.

His biographer, Mark Simpson, references what numbers among Sim's most dominant characteristics in *Alastair Sim: The Star of Scrooge and the Bells of St. Trinian's*: "...a previously dogmatic stance, swiftly circumnavigated when the moment required, into another unequivocal position—something we shall encounter on several occasions throughout his lifetime. As traits go, if does not define you as a bad person, but it does call on tolerance from those close to you."[3]

Hmmm. Sound like anyone else we know in a certain Christmas horror film? In other words: Sim was a stubborn bugger. Having pared away nose to spite his face, he would often turn to what he could move on to next and perhaps have a go at an ear.

You've probably done some math: Sim was only fifty-years-old at the time Scrooge was filmed. Dickens—and Brian Desmond Hurst to arguably even more effective ends—loaded each proverbial sleeve with an ace. Up one sleeve: the truth that Scrooge isn't ancient. In our times, when sixty is the new forty-five, or whatever it is, you can really be settling in to enjoy your life—and a long, multi-decades stretch of it—at fifty. Maybe you have some money in the bank, the kids are at school, and if that earlier marriage foundered, you have plenty of years left to meet someone else and build the union you've always wanted. Something else can go wrong again union-wise, and it's still not too late to start again. You have time—and potentially scads of it.

Sim looked older than he was—sort of. Watch his movements in Scrooge, at different emotional states of being—in the scene when Jacob Marley arrives during the carillon symphony; after the Ghost of Christmas Past travels to London town and whisks the haunted man back to Old Fezziwig's; when he recoils upon seeing his own grave; and when, after that vision—a "ha ha, fooled you!" mind fuck in extreme and in extremis—he cavorts around his much-warmer seeming bedroom than before, when he had lifted his piping salmagundi from the hob, and freaks out the maid with his joy and damn near breakdances on the day of the Lord's birth.

There is another dancing scene, too, which I will put aside for now, as you likely know exactly about which scene I am referring, and it's still too soon in our ghastly proceedings for us to dwell on expiation, gratitude, the tears of joy. Eyes, as Scrooge will imply, to truly see with, and ears to truly hear with.

What Sim does is dart. He's a high-stepper. He doesn't move with speed, but quickness. They're different. Speed wins the race; quickness is what gets you faster from point A to B when they are mere paces away from each other. It's the jump in that first stride. The jump of life. There's youth in that jump.

Sim appears to be two ages at once. His Scrooge retains the youthful capacity for wonder, which is discernible despite the moneygrubber's predilections. The dichotomy makes his transformation both believable and relatable. On a subconscious plane, he never feels too far gone to us for redemption. We identify with the character, especially in this Sim performance, because we traffic in a commodity of wish fulfillment of our own. The genius of the performance is that Sim has us understanding that he is the Everyman, without us consciously thinking that we're like him at all. That's the paradox he's tasked with pulling off, and that he is the only actor who has ever played the part who has fully done this is the reason that Sim is Scrooge as Gustave Flaubert famously remarked that he was Madame Bovary by way of a process of artistic transubstantiation.

Frank Capra's *It's a Wonderful Life* is a film that we'll see has considerable overlap with *Scrooge* when it hits pause on everything that has occurred over its first two thirds, and becomes a noir-horror hybrid. *Scrooge* is both noir and horror—with a larger emphasis on the horror, of course—and much else besides; family saga, seasonal picture, work of proto-Kitchen Sink realism, fantasy film, ghost story, fictional biopic, class study. But if we superimpose the Capra and the Hurst works at key points, there's a telling palimpsest, with top layer much like the bottom.

The two films share the same horror veins, though *Scrooge* pumps a greater quantity of blood through them. *It's a Wonderful Life* deploys the subjunctive as a narrative device— the "What if?" style of storytelling—to a greater degree than *Scrooge*, but the subjunctive features in the latter film as well, obviously—Ghost of Christmas Yet to Come and all of that—though *Scrooge* is more reliant on naturalism for its horror.

Put another way: we have the "What if?" but only after the "This is." The Marley visitation, for instance, is real. It's played as something that could have happened, that did happen. Dickens will explain certain things away. He leaves the loophole. M.R. James thought this was best with a ghost story. Create this one-percent chance that occurrences were in someone's addled brain and there alone, or the undigested bit of beef birthed the apparition.

Brian Desmond Hurst was not of a similar mind. *Scrooge* is a commitment to realness. Posterity. The reliable narrative voice. *This is how it was*. It's not a whimsy movie. The novella has a gloss of the fanciful to it. Other cinematic adaptations do as well. But I don't believe that Hurst's film is any less naturalistic than, say, Erich von Stroheim's *Greed* (1924), a touchstone of that branch of filmmaking.

Lionel Barrymore, as Mr. Potter in *It's a Wonderful Life*, is the ostensible Scrooge-figure— but only on the surface—which is apt, as he often played Scrooge in radio adaptations in the 1930s, including one overseen by Orson Welles in 1939. Barrymore was to assay the part the year before for Welles, but couldn't make it, so the budding genius who'd soon decamp for Hollywood doubled as narrator and an exceedingly Sim-esque Scrooge. You can listen to both broadcasts today, and hear how the recording with Welles in the

Sim-style—a darting quality in the voice—is the cozier production. It's also the more frightening, because we feel hermetically sealed within Scrooge's world. The lid is on tight, we can't escape.

But we also connect with Welles's Scrooge—he doesn't drive us away. (It's no coincidence that in the history of movies and radio, Welles and Sim have two of the most beckoning voices that compel our attention.) In *It's a Wonderful Life*, the viewer can't gravitate to Barrymore's Scrooge figure. He's immobile. The character is defined by a lack of even the potential of a trajectory. He is what he is, and thus he will remain.

The Everyman is not Jimmy Stewart—do you have friends like that? Know anyone who does? No, sadly, that cornucopia of kindness is too rich for most of us, out in our actual lives. The Everyperson is an Everywoman: Donna Reed's Mary Hatch/Bailey. She pulls the levers of fellowship behind the scenes, out of love, purpose, fealty, strength. She looks after people. She is a person *for others*. The ghosts are entities *for others* in *Scrooge*. Presumably they offer these services to human beings beyond the one whose case is on display here.

But Sim additionally helps us understand that behind those eyes, is a person who can also lend a hand to those around him, and for himself. They betoken in a negative direction, they betoken in a positive direction. Depending. "I fell in love with them there eyes," Billie Holiday will later sing, and the way she sings it, you know that she's speaking of Alastair Sim-type eyes. His Scrooge eyes.

This brings us to the other ace. Scrooge—particularly Sim's Scrooge—is never really that bad. We've talked about when he comes up behind the caroling children outside of his counting house and makes physical contact with them, but what is an issue of criminality, a Twitter shaming, and a lost career in our times, was merely adult-issued—and sanctioned, if you can believe it—ear-boxing at the time.

The humor we've touched on—black humor, sure, with the tart line, but humor all the same—abets this cause. The precision of the voice gives that humor added piquancy. Renders it more mordant. The humor of mordancy remains with you, follows you around—we might even say it pleasingly haunts you, to reframe M.R. James's dictum of the felicitous terror.

A Gold Medal won by Sim for his speaking prowess—the Olympics of elocution!—led to a job at a school for continuing education, plus further studies for Sim himself, resulting in a professorship at the University of Edinburgh in 1925. He tutored privately, and because of his distinctive looks, bearing, voice—and those portal-eyes—he was occasionally asked to play a role in an ad hoc play put on by a gaggle of local kids for their neighbors. I hope we'd not cast our jaundiced, twenty-first century gaze unfavorably on this now, if Sim moved among us, but he had a rapport with those younger than himself—at all of his ages—that spoke to the aforementioned inner child's capacity for wonder.

Fans of Scrooge are often aware of the trivia nugget that George Cole, who plays Young Scrooge—the debonair viper we see buddy up with Patrick Macnee's Young Marley in writer Noel Langley's inspired backstory extension—and was in his mid-twenties during filming, lived with Sim and his wife, Naomi. Sim mentored the budding actor, which Sim did a lot of, if he believed in you.

In the autumn of 1926—when he himself is the age of Young Scrooge as he all but destroys himself by turning his back on love—Sim meets the mother of Naomi Plaskitt while he is browsing in a bookstore. They are colleagues, after a fashion—she teaches poetry and diction. There's a play she'd like to enter in a local competition, but she can't find anyone to take the part of the elderly priest.

And behold, she chances upon Alastair Sim, the top of his head bald already, the King of Elocution. She offers him the role. He accepts. For weeks they rehearse at the home of the Plaskitt family. Naomi—twelve-years-old—is in the cast, and she becomes infatuated with the man performing as a priest in the family living room. When the play is performed, the contest adjudicator praises her performance, adding that the priest was downright awful. It doesn't matter. She's in love, obsessed, with Sim, and he has felt the bite of the acting bug. Six years later, they marry, with no one quite understanding the early portion of their union, beyond an undeniable bond. They remained married until his death, nearly forty-five years hence.

A lot of Sim's students wanted to be actors, so he had them perform set pieces for their grades, as if they were auditioning. He built a drama school, and when a reading given by Sim of some poems by Gordon Bottomley—quite the Dickensian name—was regarded favorably by the poet and dramatist John Drinkwater—again with the Dickensian—the elocution professor was handed a letter of recommendation that led to a casting as the Messenger in a Maurice Brown-produced version of *Othello*, with various understudy roles. And we are away in the thespian career of Alastair Sim.

For a few years, he plays on the stage in tragedies and dramas, but the real break comes with his jump to comedy, and what were called Quota Quickies. To bolster the struggling British film industry, Parliament passed the Cinematograph Films Act, which ruled that the percentage of British-made films playing in English movie houses could be no lower than twenty percent by 1937. The theatre owner had to make sure that at least 1/5 of the pictures in their screening schedule were of British origins. So, get cranking, Merry Olde England.

There was a demand for cheap pictures made fast, which meant a surplus of work to be had. Piss-taking moviegoers immediately began to distinguish between what was dubbed Quality—for example, when you went to see Capra's *Mr. Deeds Goes to Town* (1936), or a Fred Astaire/Ginger Rogers hoofer; the high-hanging fruit of American cinema—and the slummy Quota Quickies. Did you see a classy Q picture on Saturday night, or a crappy Q-squared affair?

Sim debuted in the inglorious *The Riverside Murder* (1935). You can gage the level of effort that went into many of the films by their titles. He was cast as a detective, and told to play the part as a Cockney. Sim, as he put it, "rebelled." A small rebellion, like the one we have seen Sim's Scrooge make in his countervailing of the bonhomie of Nephew Fred, his stance of "No more bread," his disavowal of what his senses have told him and what his mind knows is true as he hears the voice of his dead partner and friend (or near enough).

"I had never tried to portray a Cockney in all my life," Sim sniffed. "So I persuaded the studio to change the character into a Scot."[4]

A victory of will, then, and an obduracy that could both be useful, and not so useful. The Quota Quickies might have been largely garbage, but those featuring Sim were better than most, especially as they became funnier. That's how you would have known Alastair Sim when you went to the cinema in 1951 to watch him in *Scrooge*. The idea might have seemed a crazy one. *What is he doing in this picture, dear?* A casting completely against expectation or sense.

But what the Quota Quickies had offered was opportunity, same as a passel of ghosts, about fifteen years later. Sim's timing could not have been better. Which brings us back to someone we left screaming in his room, and a scheduled visit.

FOOTNOTES

3. This quote is to be found on p. 43 of the Simpson bio, published by The History Press in 2008. Sim's filmography was expansive and rich, even if we do mostly toast his thespian health at the Christmas season these days, thanks to *Scrooge*. Simpson is an able tour guide for those wishing to explore other Sim roles.
4. Simpson, 2008: 47.

Reel VI: This Glowing Hand

Prior to emitting his scream, and throwing himself out of his chair—into an upright, defensive posture—Scrooge listens to the sound of Jacob Marley's ghost dragging his chains over the floorboards which Scrooge himself has recently trod. There is knowledge in his gaze, as if he is cognizant of who/what approaches. It's that expression you see on the face of a loved one in a hospital waiting room when a doctor steps in to relay what everyone knows is coming, but will now be made official. Hurst and Donner cut with controlled rhythmic pace between Scrooge, the closed door, and Scrooge again, the last time—before he surges from the chair—at a rakish angle, the camera positioned on the floor, looking up at the diagonal line of Scrooge's jaw.

Fig. 5: The beholding of the ghost of Jacob Marley.

He screams as the door flies open—open door, open mouth, what Pablo Picasso would call a visual rhyme. Marley, who has clearly labored with those chains, his progress coming slowly, doesn't walk into the open doorway, he manifests, as though underscoring his ghostliness, lest Scrooge, or us, have any doubt. We already know he's a most tactile ghost, a somatic being. After some early back-and-forth, Scrooge will ask Marley if he can sit down—take a ghostly load off—and Marley will do just that. It reminds me of Ben Kenobi sitting on that swamp log with Luke Skywalker in *Return of the Jedi* (1983). The decedent aspect is maintained, amplified even by the strangeness of the sitting ghost. Immediately, Marley the ghost parallels Scrooge the man—they're each somatic, but dead.

Scrooge begins their conversation by roaring: "Who are you?" It's a full shout. Marley is implacable, and prefers to be asked who he was. Hurst leaves the camera on Scrooge, as Marley starts moving once more, the camera moving with the miser's eyes, soundtracked by those scraping chains. We thus associate the sound with Scrooge, and the chains he's been making for himself, which Marley will soon reference, adding that they're weightier than his own, given that Marley croaked seven years back, and Scrooge has nominally kept going.

Moviegoers had never before seen a ghost like this. Marley has more physical density around his head, neck, shoulders, chest—he's dressed for an evening out in swallowtail jacket and lantern sleeve with ruffle trim top—and tapers away towards nothingness at his bottom. There isn't anything hammy or contrived about these special effects. Presumably none of us know this for sure, but if the God of Reality—a Dickensian notion—told me that ghosts were real and looked as this one does, I'd say, "right-o, sir."

Scrooge whimpers, and despite the cold—his robe appears to be three-inches thick— he begins to sweat, and pulls out his handkerchief to wipe his face as he asks Marley what he wants of him. Hordern delivers the answer with a bittersweet plangency that speaks as much to his own burden as it does to Scrooge's wasted life: "Much," he says, the word all but absorbed into the preternatural ether that now infuses this room.

In other adaptations of *A Christmas Carol*, the ghost of Jacob Marley is a tool of exposition. He floats in, lays out what is to happen, gives the pros, the cons, acts as the master of ceremonies for a three-night ghost binge, but as we know, he's lying about that—it's really just one night. That's something I love about the 1843 novella: Dickens just flat out lies to you. Eh. So it goes. That's life.

This Marley must do more, because, for starters, you have one of the all-time character actors in Michael Hordern. Don't waste him. Then, there's the physical and psychological intensity that has been building as the horror components of Hurst's undertaking blend together into one of those rare works of cinema that we can identity, at any point, by any word, any still, within an instant.

Everyone knows *A Christmas Carol*, but *Scrooge* is still its own shimmering kettle of fish. As is Noel Langley's script—we'll see a lot of the pre-ghost versions of Jacob Marley in the reels to come, which you won't find anywhere else. There's the young version of

Marley, who joins Scrooge in business; the older iteration, who teams with Scrooge to take over someone else's business; and the dying Marley, who has a conversation with Scrooge that parallels the one we're experiencing now, both before (because he's not dead) and after (because we met him well prior) the fact. In Hurst's film, Marley is a foil for Scrooge, but only because of what Scrooge might yet be. The Holy Ghost can barely squeeze into that space that separates foil from dead ringer.

Hordern was Sim's junior by more than a decade, despite being the older brother figure in *Scrooge*. Born October 3, 1911 in Hertfordshire, a four-furrowed brow, receding hairline, and a nose that looked like it had been growing for the better part of a century, made Hordern appear older than his age. This served him well in the Shakespeare roles with which he was associated, King Lear foremost among them.

As with Sim, he had a stint as a teacher, and competed in drama contests as well. In 1933, upon the death of his mother, Hordern committed to the stage, with his London debut following four years after, and his film career commencing with 1943's *Girl in the News*—one of the rare British noirs at the time—directed by no less than Carol Reed.

The write-ups for *Scrooge* praised him uniformly, though for reasons I've never understood, there was a tendency to say he had a small part in the film, which is patently false, whether we're talking impact or screen time. This isn't some four-hour epic. We get a lot of Hordern, and if he doesn't "make" the picture to the degree that Sim does—and Sim makes *Scrooge* much as the Marx Brothers make a Marx Brothers picture—then we can nonetheless say that the film would be far smaller, less vatic, and not as consequential without him.

Hordern was always a reliable science fiction, fantasy, and horror story man. He remains, for many, the ultimate Gandalf, playing the role in the BBC's 1981 radio adaptation of J.R.R. Tolkien's *Lord of the Rings*. He had a face for character acting, and a voice for the radio, and I mean that as the highest compliment. For both Sim and Hordern, the speaking voice was an instrument. Mozart would write certain concertos for specific players, tailoring his music to what a specific player could do on the bassoon or what have you. When we hear Hordern and Sim speak, we feel as if a writer such as Noel Langley has adapted a text, and added on to a text, with their instruments in mind. Hordern's voice has a lower register than Sim's. When they converse in Scrooge's rooms—the same rooms where we watch Marley die later in the film, as Scrooge puts forward the cinema's leading example of poor beside manner—their voices alternate between providing counterpoint for each other, and working as lead vocal with harmony vocal. Their dialogues are not singsong, but instead sublime in their rhythmic capacity. Neither man speaks in melody, but rather rhythm.

For all of its visual derring-do, *Scrooge* is equally a verbal picture. One might think that an adaptation of *A Christmas Carol* would have to be, but Edwin Greenwood's 1923 silent version is proof for how far a director can venture with this source material sans people talking aloud. Greenwood's film is a piece of gossamer floating on a night wind. A fairy story.

Scrooge is earthen *and* phantasmagoric. We might liken it to Vincent Van Gogh's 1888 painting, *The Night Café*, with its intense tactility—benches and chairs you feel you could sit on any time you wish, by stepping into the frame—and hazy, strobing shimmer, as if we're looking at solid objects caught in the process of morphing. The corner chair is fast becoming a Circe, the absinthe bottle as Cyclopean eye.

In John Lennon's "Strawberry Fields Forever," we have a song about a real orphanage, and a song about a place that has never existed out in the world as a spot one might put in a guide book. No one talks about it this way, but that divide makes "Strawberry Fields Forever" the scariest of all Beatles songs, and also the one most nakedly outward. The work emphasizes the mind and body split, how we are oriented around different planes at once. The same applies to Jean Epstein's 1928 silent film, *The Fall of the House of Usher*, a proto-*Scrooge* in its blending of the phantasmal and the real. The accursed home itself has a ghostly hue and texture, but it still functions as a house—until it doesn't. A foot in one world, a foot in another. The borderland and the land it is thought to border, simultaneously. The same place.

Brian Desmond Hurst utilizes similar paradoxical coordinates for *Scrooge*. Our senses are heightened, we feel extreme sensitivity, but can we trust that anything is as it ought to be? Or even as it is? That's a heady concept that *Scrooge* does well: *is and not is* at once. Truth is a constant and an absolute—but perception can be a shape-shifting devil, and one who keeps us from common ground with others, and even with ourselves, as with Scrooge.

Hordern, who would die in spring 1995, helps foster Scrooge's strange ecosystem of unreal realness. An unworldly worldliness. That's the *mise-en-scène* of Orson Welles's 1948 *Macbeth*, a picture after Hordern's own heart, a kind of primordial ooze of Shakespearean thanes churning round and round within a witches' cauldron. In the ghost form of Marley, Hordern is analogous to an ambulating carving of phosphorescent light in alto-relievo. The manner of his voice provides solidity. He speaks with echo and vibrato, but the way a storyteller does, with relish (think of how Gavin Gordon as Lord Byron delivers his lines in the prelude section of James Whale's *Bride of Frankenstein*—that vim).

In 1968, managing to appear no older-looking than he did nearly twenty years prior in *Scrooge*, Hordern helped kick off what became a BBC tradition, its *A Ghost Story for Christmas* annual TV plat, with the definitive filmed version of M.R. James's "O, Whistle, and I'll Come to You, My Lad" (shortened to "Whistle and I'll Come to You"). He plays the role of the skeptic, as Sim does with this scene from *Scrooge*. In the ghostland of M.R. James, skeptics get comeuppance. That can be death, or a jolting reminder—and fresh epiphany—to get one's act together. For the Argo record label, Hordern would record no less than twenty M.R. James tales (prized on the collectors' market, and available on YouTube), and as you listen, James's tactile monsters come alive in much the same way that the ghost of Jacob Marley does in *Scrooge*, a phantom one could both touch, and put one's hand straight through—just as the words of that phantom will go straight into the man being played by Alastair Sim.

***

I recall being crestfallen as a child, in the middle of that early 1980s night, when I happened upon this scene, because I felt these men should have been friends, and were not friends. They had missed their opportunity to be close to each other. A natural way for a child to think, perhaps, with the vicissitudes of the playground—the best friend one had yesterday has moved on to another group of kids today. From the start, though, I heard a note of warning in their exchange, of wasted chances.

This is a man talking to a ghost. The ghost is terrifying. His head tilts to the side, as if his neck was snapped by a clumsy undertaker (and given that that undertaker is played by Ernest Thesiger—a veteran of *Bride of Frankenstein*, in fact, as the necrophilic Doctor

Pretorius, who enjoys hanging out in family crypts and drinking wine with a bite to eat—this strikes me as a legit possibility). In the 1971 animated version, with Sim and Hordern reprising their roles, the ghost's jaw falls to the floor when Scrooge tries to push back with the argument that maybe he's not real after all. I can only guess at the number of children who had that image infiltrate their dreams for years.

But what could have readied you for that same sequence in *Scrooge*? As Sim voices his doubts—more wishful thinking than anything—Hordern rises as Scrooge had before, every bit the ascending bolt, and uncorks a scream maintaining the theme of duality evinced throughout *Scrooge* in that this unholy ululation is human, and post-human, with the concomitant rattling of chains serving as affirming thunder (as the thunderclap after the creation sequence in Whale's *Frankenstein* acts as God's emphatic disapproval).

Fig. 6: The agony of truth.

Brian Desmond Hurst told Hordern to do what no other Marley had or would—to peel the paint from the very walls of Scrooge's room with this assault of volume. That scream takes with it any blowback Scrooge might have had. He's beaten now, and for the first time probably since those days when he was in love with Alice (played by Rona Anderson), his former fiancée, Scrooge has become what he is most scared of being: completely vulnerable. Attitudinal brusqueness cannot save him. Nor money. Or his imperiousness. His black humor. No, he will have a real human encounter, but with a ghost, because that's what his life has come to.

The horror we speak of is often visceral. This scene has no shortage of that viscerality. But it's also conceptual. It's the horror of probity and acuity, seeing exactly where one stands, without the option—which so many of us require just to carry on every day—to look away. There's terror in seeing ourselves reflected in someone else, as we are.

The ghost of Jacob Marley is the mirror in this astonishing sequence of moviemaking. That's why when the nightmare—which is also a real-life experience—has passed at the picture's end, Scrooge dances in front of his actual mirror, beholding his own image, *because now he can*. Acuity is no longer a self-directed dagger.

Another bit of trivia: during that mirror-dance scene, it's possible to detect a figure in the background, who looks oddly like Jacob Marley's ghost. Now, this was probably a grip who wandered into the shot, but I like to think otherwise, because I prefer it when horror comes full circle.

***

How long does it take us to know we have a connection with someone? True connections are rare, but we're cognizant of them within minutes. Seconds. Scrooge and Marley have the rapport of connection, but the limitations of both men precluded true friendship. In the flashback sequence that happens later in the film with Young Scrooge (George Cole) and Young Marley (Patrick Macnee), the two burgeoning lions of business agree that the world is a cruel place, and the best way to cope is to be unrelenting and unsympathetic. To arrive first at the position of command and dominance. And, in following, subjugate those on the lower ground.

The younger version of Scrooge feels a puckering of his heart as he watches the sign come down from the front of Old Fezziwig's, his former employer put out of business by these-friends-who-are-not-true friends. Bullies act this way, because bullies harbor fear. Thus, they go on the offensive. Scrooge has lived his life as a scared human. Marley's ghost no longer has fear, because it's been replaced with anguish. We fear for Marley, because he's doing Scrooge a nice turn—his goal is to help him—and Marley's anguish will last, as he says, for eternity.

I think we can agree this is harsh, but there it is—them's the rules. They may be arbitrary and disproportionate, but if you can't argue with city hall, how do you argue with the presiding forces and forms of the universe and life itself? If Scrooge had happened to die first, he'd have probably returned to his old partner in business with a warning and a thorn-studded olive branch.

Marley's soul is cooked like a Christmas goose, though he has a redeemer-by-proxy function. He's sent on missions. What he offers to Scrooge is a Faustian bargain in reverse, not that Scrooge has a say whether the ghosts will visit him. Rather than a crossroads of the Mississippi Delta that we get in American blues lore, the crossroads in question is the place Scrooge has come to in his own life.

Marley's punishment—the chains, the wandering of the earth, an inability to intercede on behalf of others (save in cases like this)—has the mephitic whiff of Dante's *Inferno* and its concept of the Contrapasso, in which the everlasting brand of meted-out justice matches whatever the dominant brand of sin had been. A thief might have his hands cut off on the quarter hour mark throughout the day, for instance. Marley circumscribed his own life. He fettered himself. Consequently, he's ballasted with his coil of chain, which Scrooge's would be even longer than, if he up and died on this given night. Marley is precise in most of what he says. How he wants to be addressed. How he sees the lit match, "notwithstanding" that he's not moving his eyes, as Scrooge waves it in front of his face. That precision may be a set-up for the one lie he tells—that Scrooge is to be visited by spirits over what's almost a half a week period. The effect would not be the same. Plus, it's better for Scrooge to have his guard down, not knowing what is actually about to happen, because then the real Scrooge has a better chance of coming out, and profiting. Morally, not financially. In the acquisition of self-knowledge, or the acceptance of this knowledge. Hordern's Marley is a masterful psychological tactician. Which makes him a pretty good friend, in the end.

Amidst its attendant fears, grave warnings—not *to the curious*, as in the realm of M.R. James, but to the incurious—the scene breaks my heart. The two men have a natural flow to their conversation, and clear détente. One thinks about what they've both missed out on, alone and together. Scrooge and Marley are each sexless beings in this Hurst treatment, which is more notable because we see them as handsome lads. Deep-dyed bachelors, made old before their time.

At parties, Nathaniel Hawthorne would relate a story about an older gentleman at the

Boston Athenaeum who read his favorite paper by the fire each day, and continued to do so, in ghost form, after he had died. The gentleman is what was called "a confirmed bachelor" in fiction and art up through the Edwardian era. The kind of man who is elderly now, but who cared only for cognac, duck hunts, vellum-bound books and the comfortable chair in which to read it deep into the night, in his thirties. They are older, these men, in ways beyond years, and they enjoy their interests.

Marley and Scrooge belong to that category, though without the willingness or the pleasure. Fear serves as motivator. To avoid pain. Loss. To have the leg up on anyone who might bring on pain or loss. Intercourse—in the sexual or societal sense—is not their interest. They are—or were—each other's lone familiar, and it has come to this, a macabre, warning/haggle session on Christmas Eve.

Hands are important in *Scrooge*. They symbolize decision and choice. Marley makes his key points with a flourish of a hand, even in his exact moment of death, when he's had a prelude of what now awaits him, and awaits Scrooge, whom he warns in his dying bed. The Ghost of Christmas Yet to Come famously points with a bony finger. Hordern's Shakespearean background serves him well; his gestures befit a lamenting Lear, thinking himself betrayed by his daughters. The calculus of Marley's argument to Scrooge is that he betrayed himself, as Scrooge is also betraying himself. The hand represents culpability. Hordern's hand will be flat, extended. Conversely, Sim folds his over his ears, his eyes, cups his head.

In the margins of another poem he would not complete, John Keats, at the end of 1819—when Young Scrooge and Young Marley were shutting down the enterprises of Old Fezziwig—wrote what would be his final work. He composed it understanding it wouldn't be read until he was dead, if ever. The lines reach out from a beyond. Reach with the hand of human connectivity, of direction underwritten with purpose:

> This living hand, now warm and capable
> Of earnest grasping, would, if it were cold
> And in the icy silence of the tomb,
> So haunt thy days and chill thy dreaming nights
> That thou would wish thine own heart dry of blood
> So in my veins red life might stream again,

And though be conscience-calm'd—see here it is—
I hold it towards you.[5]

There is a vampiric quality to the poem, which is now commonly referred to as "This living hand, but this vampire is one who self-feeds. Not the way you want to go. Keats waves us away from that outcome, and towards art and life—and the art of life—just as Marley tries to do for Scrooge. Conscience is a gift. A blessing. Not a curse. Sometimes we need a friend to help us realize this, be it a dead Keats, or a dead Jacob Marley.

If this is irony, it's the irony that comprises human life, where meaning is often sourced—when we rise to the level of seeing and grabbing it—from unlikely ledges, or in overlooked corners, or from people we had never conceived of proffering it.

Marley is nattily attired—discounting his ponderous fetters—and Scrooge is in sleeping attire. He's vulnerable. When one must face a challenge in life, it's easier when we're dressed to do so. You don't want to be in your ratty T-shirt and boxer shorts if the police knock on your door to ask if you witnessed anyone suspicious in the building earlier. I remember a football player in the NFL who'd keep his helmet on even during postgame interviews at his locker room stall. It was his defense mechanism. A barrier. Scrooge's scarf has functioned in this capacity. We may be reminded of Linus's security blanket from the *Peanuts* strips. Marley makes his take-it-or-leave it pitch to Scrooge, and to Scrooge's credit, he's willing.

His issue is his complete lack of confidence in himself, which is now out in the open. Withstanding these ghostly visitations is viewed as insuperable. He doesn't have that in him. That strength. Courage. Character. In his own view.

Marley is like Clarence in *It's a Wonderful Life*—not a guardian angle, per se, but toting a dossier of knowledge about another person that said person does not have about themselves. This is life. Thoreau's life was what it became because he understood the rarity of self-awareness, and made it his mission to discover some.

Other people often know more about us than we know about ourselves. How does one present these truths without overreaching or causing offense? A small helping of honesty can produce a lifelong rift, especially in these twenty-first century times of maxed-out sensitivity and assertions of victim status.

But Scrooge has no choice—Marley has him upon the point of a needle, with nowhere for Scrooge to go, save in the company of the ghosts. What that entails is a voyage into himself, who he has been, who he is, who he can be, if he faces the fears he's sought to avoid his entire life. Scary concept. Would anything terrify you more personally? It's up there, right?

I like to think that early on, when Brian Desmond Hurst and Noel Langley were storyboarding where they wished their film to go, that they knew they'd do what no one previously had with Marley's departure. Normally, he fizzles out, dissolves back into the dimension from which he had come, an echo of his voice intoning one last warning. But Michael Hordern's Jacob Marley will not go into that good night without a jolt of horror bookending his original appearance and the daemonic caroling of bells and clocks. "Look to see me no more," Marley states, having flung his chain back over his shoulder and making his way to the closed window of Scrooge's room. His form blends with the glass as he advances, an effect of double-diaphanousness.

The window flies open on its own accord. Marley summons Scrooge—who has been sitting in a quasi-fetal position—and the shocking scene we are about to witness initially registers on Sim's face. His eyes go wild. First they descend into his skull, then move forward, as do the eyes of crabs on their stalks. Hurst and the special effects team do not fail to deliver when we cut to the scene in the street below. Welcome to an orgy of anguish, a symphony of silently screaming ghosts crouched over a woman sitting in the snow, with no shelter, trying to warm her baby. The baby is a bundle. We don't see its head. It's suggestive of the baby in a cloth bag that Dracula throws as meat to his brides. Overlapping each other, stacked in layers—a ghostly palimpsest—the tortured beings resemble the etching that Gustave Doré did for the *Inferno* in which Charon herds sinners into a boat to cross the river Styx. They are rooted to their spots, and Charon is having a tough go of setting them on their way. They desire to remain, perhaps to make amends for transgressions, as do these ghosts in the snowy London street that Scrooge himself had walked down a portion of an hour ago. A lot has occurred in the interim.

Fig. 7: Jacob Marley takes his spot.

The arms of the ghosts sway side to side, back and forth, calling to mind the hold of a slave ship, men and women tethered to oars. They create a sort of halo space around the woman and her child, a zone in which they cannot enter, as Marley tells us. Having learned what they have learned, they want to help, and are unable to help. They did not help anyone in life. The punishment is condign, another variant of the Contrapasso.

As if this wasn't horrible enough, we get a medium shot of the woman's face—it's dirty, abraded—and then Marley disappears from Scrooge's side, sans warning and via jump cut, and takes up his place in the street below, rending, beseeching. Failing. The two men maintain eye contact, until Scrooge can take it no more. He closes the window, literally runs from the room into the bedroom where Jacob Marley died seven years ago, leaping atop the four-poster bed, and pulling the curtains shut. As if that will solve his problems.

***

Were it not for the horror that has preceded it—and a mood that is now entrenched in us with how the film has thus far gone—we might have laughed as Scrooge cinches up his bedsheets.

Were a ghost coming for me, I'd like to think I'd ready myself. Put on clothes, shoes, fortify the innards with strong black coffee. I also understand, though, what it is like to come completely apart. Lose the ability to function. Depression is this way. That's why we sleep so much as its effects take hold of us. The world is escaped via slumber. There's a link between sleep and death, as there is between depression and suicide. Scrooge puts even his head under his thick blankets, and we watch his shaking form, a lump of human residuum. The life long ago went out of his man. Just as he has tapped out on life. He feels like he has no control, so he further gives in to that feeling of impotence, powerlessness. There is no control with sleep, either, but rather the solace—if it is solace—of oblivion.

As a respite, this is the cold comfort variety. Henry Fuseli's 1781 painting, *The Nightmare*, features a slumbering woman who, though fully clothed, looks as if she's just been ravished, presumably by the simian-like, part humanoid, part troll, who sits upon her chest. Prevailing nightmare lore maintained that our worst dreams were the product of this creature in essence hopping upon your chest—bareback—and "riding" you as you slept. That is, even in the sought-for sanctuary of sleep, one had no say, and was instead acted upon.

Our problems do not go away with rest—they await us upon awaking, as soon as we come through that first, foggy patch of seconds where all is calm, and we wonder what has befallen us, what has gone wrong, before we snap back into awareness with that sinking sensation of "oh, yeah." The place in which we sleep is one which we hold as inviolable, the innermost portion of our homes, where we take to after the arduous day, where we explore ourselves sexually as young people, before anyone else does, before we trust anyone that way, or ourselves with anyone that way.

In the whole of popular music, there is scarcely a more vulnerable line than when Ringo Starr, on the Beatles' "With a Little Help from My Friends," answers the background singers' query of "What do you see when you turn out the light?" with the answer of "I can't tell you, but I know it's mine."

For the teenager, the bed is the haven of self-pleasure, where the rudimentary, early mechanics of physical love are worked out. I think we can safely assume that the middle-aged Scrooge has not passed beyond this state. He's alone in every way. Physical intimacy is foreign, depressive tendencies rampant. He has a very mixed relationship with the bed, to understate matters. There's a hospital quality in that extremes exist concurrently, and play out simultaneously. In one room, the child is born. In another, the child dies before her time.

Wes Craven's 1984 *A Nightmare on Elm Street* got its horror hook so deep into a generation of young viewers because of how it vitiated that sacred—but also earthly—space for teenagers, and also many of us, regardless of age, who know struggle. Freddy Krueger was himself a past master—a melted, ghost version of whatever that beast is in the Fuseli painting—of hitting his victims in what today we'd call a safe space. Their safest of safe spaces. Violating these sanctuaries where we let out our breath and think, "Well, at least nothing can go wrong here," is the ne plus ultra of terror. Thomas Alfredson's *Let the Right One In* (2008) is stuffed to its piranhaic gills with images and sequences of fright that incise themselves into our memories, but none more so than when a swim at the gym—benign, peaceful, rejuvenating—modulates into an attack—and subsequent rescue—of a nightmare savagery to make even the likes of Freddy Krueger go, "Damn, girl."

The battle of evil and good—the latter coming in the form of a vampire girl—plays out underwater, the effect much like when we pull the sheets over our head and seek our escape. Producer Val Lewton and director Jacques Tourneur also put a gym pool to comparable use in 1942's *Cat People*. The Lewton team had already induced so much fear in us—like the company of filmmakers to this point in *Scrooge*—that a few shadows and cat hisses piped in by the sound effects department all but deconstructs our every last nerve as we watch.

The way in which we view a pool is transformed, as a dip in the ocean would be thirty-plus-years later with *Jaws* (1975). So it goes with Scrooge and his bed. The mare—the term given to the creature in the Fuseli painting—is a rapist. We speak of consent, but depression asks for none. Fear itself can be assaultive. Anyone who has suffered from panic attacks knows how quickly the body may be overridden by that with which the mind cannot deal. The idea of "big or small" doesn't matter when we are in the grip of terror, when all is transformed. Doctors and nurses have a term for deductive overreaches. They use the metaphor of there being hoof beats off in the distance, and someone citing zebras rather than horses. Scrooge is at the place in his life where every hoof beat belongs to a zebra, every look from every passerby is meant to injure him.

In 1790, the French aristocrat Xavier de Maistre was sentenced to forty-two days of house arrest for his part in a duel. Isolated, alone with his thoughts, no visitors, de

Maistre began to see his room as he never had before. His inner domicile became transformed—or else seen as it always had been, for the first time. Struck by the conversion, he wrote a book called *A Journey Round My Room*, a work of physicality—we can all but feel the solidity of objects—but also the spectral. The hauntingly unfamiliar, in what had been a place where one thought truth was absolute, because of 1. Empirical evidence and 2. That human need for us to feel we are protected in our innermost of sanctuaries. De Maistre had a different nerve than Scrooge, because he did not live the life of the Sim character, more of which will now be revealed to us. But he came to understand how his trusted external world could dissolve on account of his mood, attitude, oppression of emotion, and subsequent shutting down of emotion.

Back to Scrooge, who we see sleeping on his back, blanket tucked under his chin, held fast by his curled hand—again with the hands and their positions—as if he is a child tuckered out after a long day. Another bell. Scrooge opens his eyes on the downbeat. They roll in his head, those eyes—side to side, up and down—as his body remains inert. He's passing through that patch of seconds that we spoke of, where we have that moment of unawareness and "wait, how did I leave things in my life?" Personally, through this part of my life, I experience those few seconds as an admixture of hope and dread. The latter prevails with Scrooge precisely as Sim's eyes turn in the direction of his room, where Marley had been.

Again, this is a highly vocal movie, but Sim's eyes are a lexicon unto themselves. Now the camera will pan over the bed—though we're still sealed within the curtains that Scrooge pulled shut—as a low murmur of strings from the Richard Addinsell score employs subtle pizzicato for a percussive effect. A drumming upon your heart.

As before, when the window opened of its own volition with the approach of Marley, so too does the bed curtain on the right-hand side of Scrooge's four-poster. I don't know about you, but if I'm in my bed, and it begins moving on its own, I scream or run. Scrooge remains. He doesn't move a muscle. Hurst trains his camera on the closed bedroom door, holding the shot for a couple extra beats. They let us know that something, or someone, is about to let itself in. Is it the right one? The wrong one? Scrooge does not have a say in this matter of admission. He doesn't grant consent. Should we have to in order to be helped?

Sometimes when I watch this film, I think that Scrooge has all but outfitted himself with one of those Do Not Resuscitate bracelets, only in the psychological and emotional sense, rather than the physical. Outfitted himself that way without honest, earnest commitment. That is, if he could start over, he'd choose to live in the active way of truly living. But starting over—and even just plain starting—is a bitch.

This has been a movie of prevailing darkness. Charcoal—glowing charcoal—has featured as the dominant color of its palette. Now, for the first time, comes the light. A ball of it, at first, a gentle infusion we can now see in front of the bedroom door. The light takes the shape of an old, wiry man. The strings have shifted to a major key, though the volume is low, because we've not reached a triumphant stage yet. We've arrived at a glimmer.

The camera cuts back to Scrooge, now leaning on his side. He dips his head—barely—in a show of respect, manners. He does not yet know what he must face, only that he'll struggle to do so. Dante pulled up to the gates of hell and encountered a placard advising all to abandon hope. Scrooge is in his own hell, but for the first time, hope is at hand. The faintness of that hope does not matter. That any exists at all, is what does. The dead hand may yet come back to life. And we are not talking zombies or vampires.

FOOTNOTES

5. Many volumes of Keats' poems don't collect this final effort, which is both sad and fitting, I think. I view the poem as existing outside of the official Keatsian body of work. That is where it belongs, in its own private pocket of meaning, between worlds. The poem is easily located online, though, at sites such as www.poetryfoundation.org.

Reel VII: Un-Oozy

If you set odds on who was least likely to make a film like Scrooge, based off of what they had done before, Brian Desmond Hurst might have been the longest of long shots. He didn't lack for praise, a consensus being that Northern Ireland has produced no finer film director, a claim I'd believe would be made even without the film for which Hurst is now known.

He was born two days before Valentine's Day 1895 in Belfast, putting him in his mid-fifties when he undertook Scrooge. He had a long life, dying in autumn 1986, though he made only eight films after Scrooge, the last of which, The Playboy of the Western World, was released in 1962.

His filmography features only about thirty works, including wartime shorts—*A Call for Arms* (1940), *A Letter from Ulster* (1942)—that display greater technical command than John Huston's more famous *The Battle of Pietro* (1945). Huston had a literary, prose-based sensibility, whereas Hurst's was more poetic, and also steeped in legend. (He excelled with treatments of the quite poetic-like prose of J.M. Synge.) He was, after all, an Irishman, and if someone could have turned one of W.B. Yeats' haunted elegies like "An Irish Airman Foresees His Death" into a film, it would have been Hurst.

Hurst knew horror firsthand. He fought with the Irish Air Rifles in WWI at Gallipoli, and in the Balkans and Middle East. In August 1915, the bulk of his outfit was slaughtered by Turkish machine gun fire in what was a massacre in all but name, the extirpation of a company of nearly 700 men. When Roman Polanski made his 1971 version of *Macbeth*, he stated to an interviewer that he understood blood better than most people. This was, of course, after the Tate-Labianca murders by members of the Manson Family. I've often wondered if what Hurst saw and survived acted as an emotional and visual codex informing Scrooge.

Like Orson Welles, Hurst learned from John Ford; but whereas Welles sat and watched *Stagecoach* forty times, Hurst, who had moved to Hollywood, hung out with Ford, talking movies, and had a brief appearance in 1928's *Hangman's House* alongside John Wayne, which was the first confirmed Wayne sighting in a Ford film. Around the time of the making of Scrooge, it's Hurst who advises Ford on *The Quiet Man* (1952), because Brian

Desmond Hurst excelled at getting Ireland right, if you will, to the last detail, even if John Ford preferred over-generalization and a lot of Blarney Stone tear-jerking.

Come the early 1930s, Hurst is in England, residing in affluent Belgravia, where he lived for the rest of his life. He harbored no resentment towards the English, though he rated them well below the level of the Irish. In 1934, the same year that Edward Ulmer gave Americans the most unhinged version of a Poe adaptation they'd ever see, with *The Black Cat*—a dark horse (kitty?) candidate for the country's greatest horror film—Hurst was also entangled in Poe, with his *The Tell-Tale Heart* being considered too gruesome for British picture-goers. It was a sound picture, but there was so little dialogue that higher-ups accused Hurst of making a silent film. *Scrooge* is verbally rich, sonorous. The words themselves—right from Peter Bull's opening narration—enfold into Richard Addinsell's soundtrack, and vice versa, but the movie's foremost energy comes from the smorgasbord of visuals.

The other forms of energy take their cues from what our eyes see. Alfred Hitchcock called this "pure cinema," and it's why a "talky" picture like 1954's *Rear Window* draws as heavily as it does on the techniques of his silent films such as *The Lodger* (1927). Prior to *Scrooge*, Hurst had produced little to suggest his masterpiece would be in the offing. There's no dry run. I wish we had a proto-*Scrooge* from Hurst, the way that Dickens presaged *A Christmas Carol* with "The Story of the Goblins Who Stole a Sexton," but we don't. You see bits and pieces—for instance, 1939's *On the Night of the Fire*, with Ralph Richardson, is a fascinating slice of British noir, predating the American *Stranger on the Third Floor* by almost a year.

Scrooge is only lightly a crime picture—if you want to count Scrooge's charwoman, Mrs. Dilber (in an inspired performance by Kathleen Harrison), nicking his curtains in the "subjunctive universe" that the Ghost of Christmas Yet to Come posits—but it often looks like noir. The shadows, the reticular constructions of black and white, the lambent surfaces of streets and building walls.

Jane Greer would joke that Jacques Tourneur—the director, as we know, of Val Lewton's *Cat People*—would light the sets of *Out of the Past* (1947)—which is as noir as noir gets—with matches. The difference with *Scrooge* is that Hurst and his cinematographer, C.M. Pennington-Richards, succeeded in finding a way to make darkness bright, if that makes sense. You turn on the TV, you catch a mere eyeful of image, and you always know it is *Scrooge* because of those blacks.

But Hurst does not arrive at a work of complete amalgamation of all that he'd done before, until he gets to *Scrooge*. It's his miraculous one-off. Which is not to discredit his steady, even innovative hand, as a maker of movies. Pressed by director/film historian Peter Bogdanovich about the checkered nature of Greta Garbo's film career, Orson Welles refused to take the bait, sagely opining that when it comes to art, sometimes one is enough—more than enough.

For Brian Desmond Hurst, that one is *Scrooge*. And it is plenty—just as the single night of visitations is all that Sim's Scrooge needs.

***

The ghost who will light out—with his light on—with Scrooge into the early days of the young Ebenezer, is played by Michael J. Dolan, who died in 1954, aged seventy. The Ghost of Christmas Past has the hardest job of any of the spirits in *Scrooge*. Marley is a lot of blood and thunder—he brings the wow factor. The Ghost of Christmas Present does a form of reportage; he's a documentarian, a broadcaster of the daily news. The Ghost of Christmas Yet to Come is working with a penitent Scrooge who just wants a second chance by that stage of the haunting game and is putty in the hands.

Memories haunt us, but what of witnessing the events of our past, the errors of our ways, as if we we had box seats for a showing of our lives at the theatre? Not only wouldn't we be protected by how we've chosen to view the past—with that creepy, oxymoronic idea of what we now call "my truth"—but we have to do this with someone sitting next to us, also seeing all. Thus, not just the horror, but the horror of embarrassment.

Fittingly, *Scrooge* was Dolan's last film. The Ghost of Christmas Past is extinguished at the end of his time with Scrooge, as with the actor who plays him. The Ghost of Christmas past is the kindest of the spirits, but he's also firm, with a tart line of reproach, but only after he and Scrooge have built up a form of relationship. It doesn't take long, and it can't—writer Noel Langley has a lot of information to pack into this portion, but he needs to be sprightly about it. *Scrooge* isn't a portmanteau in the official capacity of

Dead of Night, but it's a film likewise in parts, segments, and those parts need to have balance, including with their respective lengths. Five minutes of this, and twenty-three minutes of that, would throw off the balance of the integrated whole.

Scrooge appears willing. He doesn't rail against the ghost as he's told, while still in bed, how this will work. Scrooge has cultivated distance his entire life, but to travel with this ghost will require propinquity—they have to be touching each other. Langley uses physical proximity to hasten along the connection between these two beings. Touch is crucial. It gets them where they are going, yes, but it also brings Scrooge out. First stop: Scrooge's boyhood school, and a winter wonderland so bedecked in white, virginal snow that we might as well be in a Rankin-Bass TV special.

Fig. 8: *The snow-white purity of an Eden that never was.*

The realm of the glowing blacks has been pulled inside out. It's the Christmas holiday, and the boy version of Scrooge has been left behind, his father not wishing his presence at home, until, wait—rescue!—his sister Fanny (Carol Marsh) arrives to fetch him. George Cole, he who has been mentored by Alastair Sim, plays the younger version of Sim's character, and he listens as Fanny relays that their father is a changed man. Scrooge doesn't believe this, and we don't either; what matters is that Fanny, despite the personal difficulty, has lobbied on her brother's behalf. After all, he's not done anything, or at least nothing on purpose, save to have his mother die while giving him life.

This section of the film is Noel Langley's tour-de-force writing performance, why I assume that Brian Desmond Hurst wanted him. The above plot device—the death in childbirth bit—isn't from the novella, because there, and just about everywhere else, Fanny is Scrooge's younger sister. In *Scrooge*, she is the older sibling, and also the mother figure. After he has been cast out, she is what family Scrooge has. She is his lone connection to the kind of love that is a birthright for many. She is his protector, rather than he might have been hers as the older brother.

Marsh was another Scrooge actor with a circumscribed filmography. Hurst used either amateur or unknown actors for *The Tell-Tale Heart*, and though we'll see him go in the opposite direction here—to help the box office—he seemed to prefer this approach. Despite being in her mid-twenties at the time of *Scrooge*, Marsh plays in just four more films, one of them being Hammer's 1958 *Horror of Dracula*, as a memorably doomed Lucy Holmwood (Lucy Westenra in the novel, but *Scrooge* had already gone a long way in changing the rules for rewriting the classics).

Noel Langley himself was born on Christmas Day, in 1911. If he wasn't born to write this screenplay, he was born on the right day for it, at least. He wrote novels before he wrote for films, his breakthrough happening in 1935, with a satirical novel called *Cage Me a Peacock*, set in ancient Rome, because the Romans were so ripe for yucks.

He started producing children's books, notched a couple screenplay credits, and left London for Hollywood near the end of the decade on a seven-year contract with MGM. It was in Hollywood that Langley carved out his first slice of immortality by turning a different novel for children, by a guy named L. Frank Baum, into the screenplay of *The Wizard of Oz*. In eleven days. It was Langley's idea to use the characters who play the Tin Man, Scarecrow, and Lion feature in the sepia sequence that begins the film (and concludes it), creating a frame story, and to switch the color of Dorothy's slippers from silver to ruby.

Can you imagine watching *The Wizard of Oz* and not seeing ruby slippers? Further changes were made without his knowledge, so that when Langley sat by himself at midday in a Hollywood theater and watched the picture, he cried tears of dismay and regret. What he called "cutesy and oozy" elements had been introduced. The work had not pushed as hard in the direction he wanted it to. But *Scrooge* would—boy would it ever, and not even the gimlet eye of Noel Langley could discern any evidence of "cutesy and oozy," when all had been said, and all had been done.

DEVIL'S ADVOCATES

***

The works of Charles Dickens are the secret weapon of British horror prior to the Hammer boom that kicked off in 1957 with *Curse of Frankenstein*. There were precious few other fright-fest quality pictures to speak of. At the peak of the pile, you'd find the movies starring the always over-the-top Tod Slaughter, such as *Sweeney Todd: The Demon Barber of Fleet Street* (1936) and *Crimes at the Dark House* (1940), a super loosey-goosey adaptation of *The Woman in White* (1859) by Wilkie Collins, who had been Dickens' confederate in assorted literary matters.

The Slaughter movies were manic melodramas, with a glaze of the Grand Guignol. It wasn't until David Lean directed *Great Expectations* (1946) and *Oliver Twist* (1948) that British horror started to scratch out a legitimate toehold. The horror was not overt, because the horror resided in the atmosphere of these films, with their baleful moors and workhouse deprivations (which Scrooge laughs off), rather than their plots. The horror feels incidental, not primary. It isn't the thrust—more like a bonus, and a suggestion to a writer like Langley, and director Hurst, that the full monty of horror existed in Dickens, if you were willing to carve it out and erect a display for your audience.

Langley is the perfect writer for *Scrooge*, and in the following year of 1952, he also wrote the screenplay for *The Pickwick Papers*, and directed the film himself. As Dickens' first novel, *The Pickwick Papers* was a collage work, jammed with tales and ghost stories. The Langley picture buttresses *Scrooge* nicely, a sort of sister, follow-up with a considerable fear quotient. As with *Scrooge*, *The Pickwick Papers* was made for Renown, and produced by George Minter. Hermione Baddeley—a winsome, devoted, but borderline-acidulous Mrs. Cratchit in *Scrooge*—is pressed back into service. The movie is another comprising the pre-Hammer backbone of post-war English horror. If you've read the novel, you know it's also a free-for-all of form. Seemingly anything Dickens could think of went into the pot. It doesn't lend itself to the formulation of a taut screenplay, but Langley was unlike anyone writing movies at the time, or conceivably ever.

He was a literary man himself, who had no problem slicing and dicing someone else's text in the past, no matter how canonical it may have been perceived as—Langley didn't stand on ceremony, and he wasn't intimidated by other authors. In today's literary climate of MFA programs and their prescriptive heterodoxy, Dickens would have a hard time with *A Christmas Carol*. It's social realism, yes, which is what is presently insisted upon by a literary caste system that is killing off reading, but social realism via the otherworldly. There's no navel-gazing, no fictionalized autobiography. It's a work of pure, dauntless imagination.

Were he writing now, I think Dickens could mount a battle against hidebound literary mores, but he might also choose to aim *Carol* towards the Young Adult market. L. Frank Baum did just that with his Oz novels and stories, and there is horror a'plenty in the 1939 film. It's a wonder that Judy Garland's Dorothy isn't scarred for life when she awakes once more— just as Scrooge does—in the bed where her adventure began.

When the tornado sends Dorothy's house skyward, spinning in cyclonic fury, she looks out the window, as people she knows drift by, including Margaret Hamilton as Miss Almira Gulch, and soon to be the Wicked Witch of the West.

Look at the overlap with the street scene in *Scrooge* as Marley joins the ranks of the undead who are unable to aid the homeless woman with her child. Did the idea come from Langley? It's a safe bet. *The Wizard of Oz* was supposed to be family fun, but do you find those flying monkeys easy on the nerves? A house landing on a nefarious witch and crushing her to death, but leaving the feet sticking out? (Those dangling feet are the creepiest detail.) How about a witch melting before our eyes? The film gave kids nightmares, and adults the willies.

Every other version of *A Christmas Carol*—with the exception of the 1984 version by *Scrooge* editor Clive Donner—is done in what I think of as good fun. Any scares are mild, even risible. We're not to take them seriously. Everything will be fine in the end. The 1971 animated version is the cartoon extension of *Scrooge*, and neither makes us feel for a second that anything will be at all fine in the end, until we get closer to it.

That's Langley's script, and its unwillingness to merely kick a Christmas present our way. As the Frankenstein monster was shocked into life, so too will *Scrooge* shock us into awareness about our own lives. In relating to Sim's characterization of Scrooge, we watch him watch his past, as we reflect upon our own. How would we feel if we had to revisit three defining moments that had made us who we were? Or—and this is the horror rub—kept us from whom we might have been, and who we can still be, if we pull a Scrooge, so to speak, in our own way?

The sequence with the Ghost of Christmas Past moves with alacrity. There's no dilation in Langley's script. The pace is up-tempo, but to put matters in the terms of Scrooge's bed sheets, we're talking a high thread count here. That is, a lot of detail.

Langley extends Scrooge's backstory—but he doesn't embellish it. This is some seriously ballsy screenwriting. We witness Scrooge witnessing—as a spectator, rather than participant—three life events that have to rip the soul out of him. The first is the scene at the school, with Fanny.

"You must live forever, Fan," Young Scrooge says to his sister, on account that no one else loves him, and he needs somebody. The stark reminder of aloneness—where it begins—is out in plain view for Scrooge, alongside the Ghost of Christmas Past, to experience all over again, but knowing what he now knows, having lived as he's lived, with his death-in-life style of existence. That is one bucket of cold water tossed over the human heart.

There's a beautiful bit of deep focus photography when we see the lower half of an attendant outside the window, shouting into the dormitory for someone to bring down Master Scrooge's trunk. Hurst is playing off another moment of deep focus photography in Orson Welles's *Citizen Kane*, when young Welles—just like we have Young Scrooge—is seen playing outside in the snow, shouting "the Union forever!" as his mother signs him over to the guardian who will take him away, just as Scrooge's father has in effect signed him away.

Fig. 9: Brother, sister, depth of field.

The verbal irony cuts us to the quick. In both scenes, a family unit—with the matriarchal concept at the fore—is dissolved, or about to be. As Young Scrooge and his sister embrace, and the trunk is loaded on the carriage, composer Richard Addinsell interweaves the melody of the Scottish ballad "Barbara Allen," originally published in 1740. The melody becomes Fan's theme, as well as Scrooge's canticle of darkest horror, and saving light. So much of *Scrooge* cuts both ways. Faced fear turns that fear into peace. Scrooge has a way to go. As for the lyric of "Barbara Allen":

> It was in and about the Martinmas time
> When the green leaves were a falling
>
> That Sir John Graeme in the west country
> Fell in love with Barbara Allan
>
> O hooly, hooly rose she up,
> To the place where he was lying
>
> And when she drew the curtain by,
> "Young man, I think you're dying."

Samuel Pepys, in a diary entry from January 2, 1666, associated the song with the Christmas season. Bells feature in the lyric—a woman who had rebuffed this Sir John Graeme over a perceived slight, is reminded of him, after his untimely death, each time the church bells toll.

And as we know, *Scrooge* loves its bells. Richard Addinsell builds them into his score, interpolates their clangor within the middle of traditional Christmas carols, shattering our expectations as per seasonal musical airs and helping to make *Scrooge* a film for all seasons. "Barbara Allen" is a brilliant, unexpected choice. We even get bed curtains, and a man dying in bed. Scrooge is dying in his bed emotionally, psychologically, spiritually, rather than physically, but the point holds.

After the scene at the school, we're bequeathed a repose: vigorous dancing at the kitted-out workplace of Old Fezziwig (a made-for-the part Roddy Hughes). The dancers are packed in tight (which makes the depth of field achieved by Hurst and Pennington-Richards extra-striking), and I am not aware of a scene of greater joviality anywhere. The joy contrasts with what we know about Scrooge, and what we're now experiencing firsthand from his past. Old Scrooge—that is, Alastair Sim—dances in place. We're happy for him, but also gutted—again, the juxtaposition with the life set so deep in its ways.

Fig. 10: Fezziwig, lord of the dance, before young Scrooge and Marley put him out of business. More deep focus.

We've talked about how Sim darts. He darts physically, and his sentences can dart about, too—he's an agile, balletic speaker. *Scrooge* builds a lot of its terror via that idea of comparison. What could be. What is. What once was. What now is not. The dancing, the darting is crucial, always suggesting the idea of movement in our minds as we watch the film. For horror to have maximum purpose—beyond "gee, that was frightening"—it also requires release. That release is not the same as a happy ending. But the vise must be opened and the audience allowed to view whomever it was who had been ground down, tested, tortured perhaps.

Movement—the darting—is paramount to that release in *Scrooge*. Throughout almost all of the film, Scrooge undertakes movement of that darting nature when he's fleeing, cowering, generally wants to die, or when he's shuffling back and forth at Old Fezziwig's, which is bittersweet. He's not really dancing with these people. There's no joining in, as the Ghost of Christmas Past reminds him. At best, he has simulacrum. Another form of existence, sans life.

***

Richard Addinsell, born January 13, 1904, in London, had been writing film music for almost twenty years, before his dalliance with *Scrooge* and his ghosts. Addinsell was a percussive writer, by which I mean, his music clangs, it hits hard in its rhythmic intensity. He rattles and rages. Hurst had worked with Addinsell before. These three men—Langley, Addinsell, Hurst—are the Murderers' Row of what I think of as management level talent behind *Scrooge*. The ace front office staff.

Alastair Sim represents the star player upon the pitch, with notable assists from his teammates, but in the composer, writer, and director, we have a Dream Team. They're akin to the band avant-garde post-bop pianist Andrew Hill assembled for his groundbreaking 1964 album, *Point of Departure*. The run of that band was short-lived, as with the creative team behind *Scrooge*, but everyone knew exactly what they were doing and attempting to bring off.

Hurst's 1941 film, *On Dangerous Ground*, was about a shell-shocked combat pilot who had previously been a virtuoso concert pianist. Flashbacks are utilized, as they are in this Noel Langley-driven sequence in Scrooge, though without the nuance. Producer William Sistrom wanted to hire Sergei Rachmaninoff to write the central musical work of the film, but he declined. The offer then went to Addinsell, who composed the sonically assaultive, nerve-jangling *Warsaw Concerto* for which the movie is now best known. Actually, Addinsell's piece all but exists autonomously, a work of musical art that hardly anyone associates with the movie it was written for, a la "Stella by Starlight" from Lewis Allen's 1944 haunted house film, *The Uninvited*. *Warsaw Concerto* is to classical/film music as Jimi Hendrix's "The Star-Spangled Banner" is to rock and roll. It's a fusillade of notes, and the piano is attacked so vigorously that to play the work well is to play the piano such that it becomes out of tune. Addinsell's score beats the hell out of the instrument. The piece is thrilling, the volume outrageous. Punk classical piano, by way of post-bop, feedback, and Free Jazz, part Cecil Taylor, part Beethoven's *Hammerklavier* sonata, part Jelly Roll Morton's "The Finger Breaker." Thematically the concerto recreates post-traumatic stress, an attack leading to a person becoming broken, and then trying to live after the fact of that fracturing.

Addinsell worked for Sam Wood (1939's *Goodbye Mr. Chips*), David Lean (1945's *Blithe Spirit*), and Alfred Hitchcock (1949's *Under Capricorn*), but they brought out a gentler side, which may have led to one critical conclusion that he wrote in the "English Light Music" style, which will cause any *Scrooge* fan to declaim, "As if!" Addinsell's Scrooge score gravitates towards the atonal. He might as well be Steve Reich, or *Ascension*-era John Coltrane. A melody like that of "Barbara Allen" is used as a leitmotif, and a highly euphonic variety at that, but damn does this score rattle some bones. It is Addinsell's music—before anything else—that signposts to us that we've come to a place of terror. Even before the movie itself truly begins. We see the Renown Pictures Corporation card, then Addinsell gets to work with bulky chords in the brass that simultaneously slash and detonate as a hand—as ever in *Scrooge*—reaches into the first frame to select *A Christmas Carol* from a tidy shelf of Dickens books.

Guttural piano chording follows, with an echo effect creating even greater density. Throughout the film, Addinsell employs a technique in which he uses a Christmas carol, then cracks it open with a discordant barrage of atonality. We like Christmas carols, generally speaking, because they're almost always in minor keys, but they're not downbeat. A song in a minor key that nonetheless feels uplifting is a song with a knack for staying within our memory, seeming to be both true-to-life and as if it has come from some shadowy, mysterious, maybe not wholly-human dimension. Addinsell writes in a way similar to jazz musician Thelonious Monk, a composer whose works are best listened to at night, in darkness, with their built-in indigo moods, and minor keys resulting in music that's somber, but not too somber—hopeful, if not happy. The music of post-twilight times, both literally and figuratively.

After our "break" at Old Fezziwig's, we're told to turn and see Ebenezer Scrooge in love, with the comely Alice (Rona Anderson). Woo is pitched, pertaining to an engagement ring. Young Scrooge has no issue with poverty. He's poor, Alice is poor, they are each happy. As George Cole's Young Scrooge makes his pledge of eternal love, Alastair Sim's Scrooge turns to the Ghost of Christmas Past, saying that he has seen enough. We know that this moment marks the apogee of the relationship. The descent follows, the pain, which is self-generated. The scenes with the Ghost of Christmas Past take the form of Scrooge shriving to a holier being. A confessional, but a reluctant fessing up on Scrooge's part. The reluctance is related to fear. We watch as this romantic relationship ends, when it need not end. When nothing positive—for Scrooge—comes of that ending.

Later we'll see Alice married to someone else whom she deserves, who deserves her, and I don't think we can overstate the torment Scrooge endures in these scenes. What could be worse than reliving the breaking of your own heart, which you were complicit in, because of your failings? Your cowardice? Your selfishness?

The scene when Alice returns her ring to Young Scrooge, leaving his life forever, packs as much fear as Jacob Marley's visit had, or when the Ghost of Christmas Yet to Come clues Scrooge in to his final outcome—in a parallel world—of dying alone and unloved. Or more fear. In film noir, there's the device where the doomed anti-hero has to make a decision, and what he decides seals his fate. In *Scrooge*, this is that film noir moment of fate-sealing. Scrooge believes as much. He's witnessing what is tantamount to an absence of hope. The stitch in time when all hope was removed for one man. This man, who has gone on in the time since merely because, well, what the hell else was he supposed to do? Kill himself?

The Ghost of Christmas Past emotionally KO's Scrooge throughout their time together. Scrooge is struggling to withstand the blows and get up again—fight another day. I think that's why this ghost is the kindest to him, at least outwardly. We're cognizant of the empathy the ghost has for Scrooge. The ones that follow won't show any. But in Scrooge's dark night of the soul, this is the trickiest leg of the journey.

Noel Langley gives us a series of scenes featuring Young Scrooge in business, with an offer to leave Fezziwig's and join the employ of Mr. Jorkin, whom you won't find in the Dickens novella, because he exists solely in Langley's script. Jorkin is played by Jack Warner, a useful actor to have, even in a small role, because he drove the box office. The scenes are vignettes, but they're fully developed, too. Let's call them full flashes.

We're moved with brisk pace between these scenes, transitioning via an hourglass that travels down what I assume is some wormhole of time. People make jokes about this hourglass, terming it clunky. But wipes and dissolves wouldn't work, because we're hopscotching in time, and a wipe or dissolve can also mean "later that day!" or "meanwhile, in this part of town."

But that hourglass is never more deadly than when Scrooge and ghost arrive in the room where the former's sister, Fan, is dying. Again, we're treated to the brilliance of Noel Langley. Remember, Fan is the older sibling. This isn't the novel. "No, spirit, not here," Scrooge begs. Sim's voice quavers. You can hear the fight empty out of him, as he realizes—even as we're not fully out of the wormhole, with Fan's wan face beginning to coalesce into focus—where the ghost has taken him. "Yes, here," the ghost answers. The words are necessary, the visit necessary, but I understand how one might watch this scene with a hand over the eyes, fingers barely spaced apart, as we do in other movies when the horror becomes too much.

Young Scrooge sits bedside, leaning over his sister as death advances upon her. He's on the same side of the bed as he soon will be, in the forthcoming flashback, when Jacob Marley dies and Sim is the Scrooge who bears witness and the Scrooge who is witnessed. But first it's George Cole in the hot seat. It's a tight shot, almost a joint close-up. The scene is so intimate that we assume no one else is in this room.

Cole/Scrooge tries to deliver a pep talk, that the situation is not as dire as Fan thinks, and she'll recover. He's saying the words as much for himself. They have a selfish component, but we pity this man all the same. He believes no one else loves him but this person, a sister who was also champion, friend, and maternal figure. A doctor—in soft focus—walks behind the chair in which Scrooge sits. He busies himself with a basin or some such—something medical—on a table.

Fig. 11: Sibling death tableaux.

The doctor is careful to remain in the background, to not encroach upon this last visit. We don't expect the cut that comes. Hurst shows us the bulk of the room now, from where the door is, with a man's back taking up most of the left side of the frame. The doctor, on the right, is no longer visible. Scrooge ministers to his sister, his hand on the bed near her breast, lips near her forehead, as if about to kiss it. Everything is in focus. Foreground, background. The doctor walks into the frame—all of this occurring as the soundtrack plays the "Barbara Allen" melody at low volume and a slower tempo—and puts his hand on Scrooge's shoulder.

We don't know where Sim/Scrooge and the Ghost of Christmas Past are standing/floating, just that they're here. The hand on the shoulder is meant to convey, "Okay, my poor fellow, that's enough, come away." I don't know how to say this, other than to say what happens next fucks me up. The scene has asked a lot of us as viewers. You have to endure it. We can only wonder how Scrooge—who has also been watching as we've been watching, out of view—is not howling like some dying animal. Young Scrooge rises from the chair. He's in a fog. His eyes focus on the ground, as he walks as one does in a daze. But he looks up as he nears the man standing in front of the door.

This is his brother-in-law, of course. As Scrooge is about to say something—and we know from the look that is now in his eyes that his words will be ferocious—the cry of a newly born child comes from the corner of the room to the man's left, which is out of our view. The child is Nephew Fred, whose birth results in the death of his mother. Young Scrooge draws a sharp intake of breath, and for a second, we think he might punch the man standing in the door. But this man—showing strength and selflessness—after all, it's his wife—reaches for Scrooge, to comfort him. Repulsed by his touch, Scrooge pushes the man away, and storms from the room. One unknown corner of the bedroom remains, and Hurst cuts to it now. We know who we'll see there.

"How could you have brought me here?" Scrooge asks the ghost. "Have you no mercy? No pity?"

But we're not done. Young Scrooge had left that room thinking his sister was dead. She was not dead. Which is to say that Scrooge never actually saw her die. And now, older Scrooge will see what his younger self did not.

I'm not sure how you out-horror this scene, frankly. There are no monsters. No vampires. No gore. The ghost on the scene is a spectator, not an agent of fear. The horror is the horror of humanness. Of the business of life, or the business end of life. Which is not a commercial proposition. This is also the horror of a failure to endure. A horror of giving in. Of becoming un-whole. And remaining that way. It's the horror of Scrooge, and the most relatable horror of *Scrooge*.

"Ebenezer," comes the faint voice of Fan from the bed. "Promise me you'll take care of my boy," she says, and expires, as the melody of "Barbara Allen"—Langley, Addinsell, Hurst, working in brilliant accord—becomes pronounced. On the very note of death, we hear muffled kettle drums, in 2/4 meter, a march. Times marches on. Life marches on. Some are left behind, including the living. The Ghost of Christmas Past says all that he can say: "You heard her." He's remonstrative, but gently. And all that Scrooge can do is beg for forgiveness. His voice rises. As it increases in volume, it becomes increasingly tremulous, until Scrooge covers his face with his hands, and weeps. Look ever-so-closely, and you will see the ghost nod.

There's more to come with the tour of the life that had been. Scrooge and Marley meet. They put Old Fezziwig out of business. The official break-up that we already knew was coming between Scrooge and Alice is enacted. After that, we say goodbye to Young Scrooge and Young Marley. Michael Hordern returns, and we're pleased to have him. Prior to Langley, Jacob Marley the man was as much a vague rumor as a person. *Scrooge* is the lone work that gives him true dimensionality.

As various men of business—an association of sorts—sit around a table, presided over by Mr. Jorkin, a threat of scandal and potential blackmail hangs in the balance. The exact nature of the crimes is not adumbrated, but they don't have to be. What matters is that Scrooge and Marley have these rivals by the balls.

For most of the scene, Hordern has a look on his face of the well-fed cat. You can imagine canary feathers sticking out of his mouth, his hands clasped over his belly. Sim is languid-eyed, as if these people represent pure tedium to him, and deserve what they have coming. He fingers his watch watch fob, until the moment when it's time to speak, and Scrooge and Marley make their power grab. They're in lockstep with each other. Symbiotic. Watching them together in this film, you think it would have been so easy for their fates to have been reversed. That is, Scrooge's possible salvation also rests on the order of death. A caprice of the universe? Or the business end of life?

We've been moving around through so many points in time that Hurst has to situate us closer to the present day. Langley's key additions to the Dickens novel are in the reels with the Ghost of Christmas Past. These new elements were a risk—everyone else who adapts *A Christmas Carol* opts for the more conservative route—but they've paid off, so long as Scrooge can be deposited back in his rooms, and there may follow a natural trade-off to the Ghost of Christmas Present.

After Sim and Hordern, Kathleen Harrison as Mrs. Dilber, Scrooge's charwoman, is the next most important player in *Scrooge*. There's a reason she's listed high up in the credits. Everyone knows that in the end, Scrooge helps the Cratchit family. Their handicapped son, Tiny Tim, does not die, and has this new avuncular presence in his life. Mrs. Dilber, though, is the character closest to Scrooge by dint of her job. She's the one who goes into his home. Who knows him better than Bob Cratchit or Fred do. And, what do you know, Mrs. Dilber is another Noel Langley invention.

She ties much of the film together, and we're shown what she would have become had Scrooge not undergone his transformation, as she robs his home following his death, in the alternate reality suggested by the Ghost of Christmas Yet to Come. In *It's a Wonderful Life*, Clarence the Angel is thorough in his case to George Bailey about the lives he impacted. Saved. Transformed. Mrs. Dilber might have been saved herself by Scrooge. We can draw that inference when watching the interaction between the two after Scrooge awakes on Christmas morning. For now, though, she races down that same alley where Scrooge had bumped the caroling children, to let Bob Cratchit know that Jacob Marley is about to die, and that the clerk should inform his master of this imminent demise. Scrooge can't delay if he wishes to have a final word. The Scrooge who sits bedside this time is unrecognizable from the one who had leaned over Fan.

Same alley, same counting house. Same apartment stairs, but they belong to Jacob Marley. Same bedroom. Same bed? Creepy. But I wouldn't put it past Scrooge. Would he have even changed the sheets? The script grounds us in the familiar, after showing us much that was new, and new to Dickens. We know these places, the imagery, but the narrative laid atop the scenery is fresh.

Ernest Thesiger's undertaker—Mr. Stretch, the ultimate in undertaker names—waits for Scrooge outside of Marley's door, literally rubbing his hands together, as if he can't wait to squire away another corpse.

"You don't believe in letting the grass grow under your feet, do you?" Scrooge says with a chuckle.

This is a hardened man. Ossified, as though he is not made of flesh and blood.

"Ours is a highly competitive business, sir," Mr. Stretch replies through tightly pursed lips that round up into a smile.

Scrooge asks Mrs. Dilber if Marley is dead yet, the way we might ask if the shrimp is fresh at the super market. Without waiting for an answer, he enters the room himself.

Marley doesn't have a lot to say. Scrooge makes token conversation ("Are they seeing to you properly?"). He couldn't be less interested. There's a last Langley kicker coming, and I bet Dickens wished he had thought of it himself: Marley, with a final breath, tells Scrooge to save himself. We can look at it this way: Marley has seen what awaits him. He's not dead, but he's been made aware of his forthcoming punishment. The world of the living and the dead overlap, in some cosmic estuarial capacity. The idea, once more, of duality. Scrooge, as we know, is technically alive, but really dead. He and Marley parallel each other until the last—or Marley's last.

Marley's final movement is a flutter of his hand. "I hold it towards you," Keats had written, to haunt the days and chill the dreaming nights, for those in need of both. Where Marley dies, Scrooge awakens. He's closer to the end of the tunnel than he knows. But a tunnel of life, or death?

Fig. 12: Marley reaches out to Scrooge with a dying hand.

Reel VIII: He Returneth and He Danceth By

The boy who arose in the middle of the night, visited by the ghosts of his dreams, anxieties, fears that he'd be taken from his home, never to return, sat and watched *Scrooge* until its pre-dawn conclusion. When he returned upstairs and got back in his bed, he did so cloaked in a sensation of peace, which was both strange and not strange, because the film had scared him, while also offering an embrace of comfort. The boy felt that the movie was loyal to people like him, who were uneasy in the ways that Ebenezer Scrooge was uneasy, even in this junior, kiddie version of a boy. All had come out well, and what means had procured that wellness? They had come from within the man who the boy did not yet know was played by someone named Alastair Sim, though he'd learn this soon enough, thanks to some research in the basement of a local library. A man had decided to trust himself as a way to get better at trusting others. That night, the boy made a similar decision. He never told his parents about what he had seen in what he viewed as an essential violation of a kind of in-house curfew, but not because they would have been angry. He just wanted to have a secret between him and a movie. It wasn't like Scrooge ever turned to Bob Cratchit one day at work and said, "Let me tell you, my good clerk, there was this night when the ghost of Jacob Marley came to me, and you won't believe what else went down!"

That night from my boyhood remains my own Christmas Past interlude with Scrooge. I love Christmas, and *Scrooge* is the holiday in movie form to me, but my mind has articulated a pointed thought over years of watching the film and sensing this thought, but not always giving it conscious voice: Scrooge is also not a Christmas film at all. Yes, Christmas is in evidence. But Cratchit is only getting a day off. The Ghost of Christmas Past and the Ghost of Christmas Yet to Come do not focus on Yuletide doings. There's dancing at Fezziwig's—that's about it. One can watch this film in April, August, or the lead-up to Halloween, and it slots in no less cozily than it does on December 20, with snow blowing outside, and the mulled cider ready for quaffing. We can't say this about any other version of the Carol. Christmas is ancillary in what is the definitive Christmas film. Again, the duality.

The final two ghosts, and the peroration portion of the movie, in which we view the man who is now changed, happen fast. Not too fast—but they have a home stretch vibe.

The ursine Francis De Wolff plays the Ghost of Christmas Present. Scrooge is intimidated by his sheer size, upon awaking once more after having taken to his bed. The travels with the Ghost of Christmas Past understandably tuckered him out. Unlike his earlier slumber following on from the visit of Jacob Marley, this one seems healthier—a recharging rather than retreating. The Ghost of Christmas Present is a cheat. He presents this smiley, happy façade, but of all the ghosts who speak, he's the real hard-ass, with a cruel streak.

He has contempt for Scrooge, which isn't hidden well at all. The forest-like beard and festive robe—what a costume—misdirect our expectations. Scrooge lets down his guard, and he's chatty with this ghost, asks him questions about his family, his job description. Scrooge as investigative reporter is an arresting concept, because this ghost shows Scrooge what is tantamount to the news of the day that no one sees—the news of families, as their attendant dramas and lives play out behind closed doors.

There's a blazing fire in Scrooge's hearth, with hogsheads of ale and overstuffed barrels of fresh fruit all about the place. I imagine Hurst saying to his set dressers, "Make it look like ultimate Christmas!"

Scrooge minces towards the ghost, a delicate, submissive creature, but one who advances of his own free will. Scrooge doesn't propose a plan to bail out, go back to bed. He's willing. He wants the journey. Given what we've seen this Scrooge subjected to—which is more than what Dickens asked the original Scrooge to witness—he earns respect. Ours, definitely. And though he's about to be shamed—the Ghost of Christmas Past would make an excellent internet-era Social Justice Warrior—he's had an accession of self-respect.

The ghost and Scrooge set to soaring, with a first stop in a mining village straight out of Zola, the miners and their families huddled around a hearth that is larger than Scrooge's—his Christmas glow, if you will, is still in development—and voicing a rendition of "Hark! The Herald Angels Sing." Hurst moves his camera in a slow dolly shot, inching closer to the faces. Composer Addinsell uses this carol throughout the film. It features as a song he splits in two, fracturing the melody so that a few seconds of atonality may bubble forth.

The thematic core of the song is tolerance, expressed as "mercy mild." Tolerance means openness. Think of where this carol features most prominently in our pop culture: with *A Charlie Brown Christmas* (1965), for instance, an animated special about a boy who is frequently derided. He can do no right in the perceptions of those who know him. Until they curb their own judgment.

It is "Hark! The Herald Angels Sing" that takes us into full-fledged nightmare mode in *It's a Wonderful Life*. As George Bailey comes undone—going so far as to ask his wife why they ever had children—in front of those children, no less—his daughter sits at the piano, pecking out the melody, again and again. That melody—and the message of the song—bores into the viewer's skull, but in a background way, because the focus is on Bailey. The meaning is primary, but the music itself is incidental. The sound comes from the home, not a studio setting of professional musicians. Diegetic sound. Addinsell also travels down the diegetic road with these caroling miners, the result being an immediacy where the viewers are as much grounded in a dominant "newness"—this present—as Scrooge himself is.

It's sunny and snowing hard as Bob Cratchit walks to his home with Tiny Tim (Glyn Dearman) upon his shoulders. Dickens' *A Christmas Carol* could well be a perfect work of art. I think *Scrooge* is, too, and forced to choose one over the other, for the Valhalla of art, I'd opt for the movie. But the closest the novella has to a weak link is the Tiny Tim character, a maudlin, lachrymose construction that I think Dickens tossed out there as a holiday sop. Paradoxically, in just about every film version of the Carol, even those that are checkered at best, Tim works as a character. He beholds the world with wonder, and a wisdom beyond his years, which doesn't come across as efficaciously on the page. He keeps people honest, holds them to a standard they might not have met on their own.

The scene at the home of the Cratchits is warmly lit. When there's been light in this movie, it come from aggressively elemental forces—fire, for instance. Soft light bathes this room, with its light plaster walls. Scrooge has to listen to Mrs. Cratchit trash his name, but he can't blame her. Bob rallies to Scrooge's defense, a defense of pity. He has what Scrooge does not, for all of the money Scrooge possesses in the bank. He would like, if possible, to share his form of largesse. The knowledge of that pity, that desire to intercede, which had been denied to the dead Jacob Marley and his ghostly cohorts in the street outside of Scrooge's house, registers on Sim's face as a wide-eyed stare. The eyes double as a desire to reach, connect, embrace—bridge the expanse.

When we get to Nephew Fred's place, the warm lighting effect is continued, though it's now later in the day. The sun has gone, and a party with dancing and games is being had. Scrooge is the punchline for a joke, but the joke, too, evinces pity, not hardness. The well-fed Mr. Tupper (Richard Pearson), a friend of Fred's and decidedly a hale fellow well met, has few lines in this film, but this veritable stranger to us—because we're not long in his company—performs one of the most generous acts of simple human kindness in all of cinema. For now, he flirts—with a woman who seems out of his league—and takes up his part in the word-play game. Hurst makes us know this man with just a few quick brushstrokes, so that we will remember him. One of the challenges *Scrooge* poses to us isn't just to do right by friends and family, or those we hope to become close to—but anyone in need. Doing right by those we do not know, acting as their keeper, may outweigh all. Or, if there's a point above all points to life, that's most likely it.

Speaking of which: Have a guess what Scrooge's ex Alice is doing with her Christmas holiday? She's at a church-run charity hospital for the poor and sick in the next scene, tending to their needs. Scrooge walks over to her, comes as close as he can to touching this woman he's not known for several decades, asking the ghost if she is real or shadow? He knows the answer without the ghost supplying it. "Did you not cut yourself off from your fellow being, when you cut yourself off from that gentle creature?" the ghost responds, and what can Scrooge say? Of course he did. So he says nothing, and Hurst takes us back outside. The scenes of the present have been internal scenes. Caroling miners, the Cratchit house, Nephew Fred's home, the alms station. Domesticity, succor. Various forms of bread-breaking and health-drinking. The Ghost of Christmas Present has put in the odd acerbic comment or two. He's an eye-on-the-scene reporter—the vignettes have the quality of news reports—but he's also a critic working on a bad notice. In slasher films, there's the moment of calm, before the blade-wielding maniac leaps out of the brush, and beheads two handsy teens. The moment is so familiar that it's been lampooned and aped for the better part of a half century. You wouldn't expect that moment in *Scrooge*, but it's here, only set-up so well that we have no idea that not only is it coming, but a double-whammy of "WTF, man" horror is about to squash us against the backs of our chairs.

The Ghost of Christmas Present doesn't utilize the egg-timer-through-the-wormholes-of-time transitory device of his predecessor; dissolves through a fustian blanket of haar are preferred. And so through the fog we come, to stand in the darkened streets of London, those glowing blacks that have been so familiar to us now restored. The duo have reached their parting moment, which occurs when the ghost opens his robe, exposing two unwashed, cowering, children at his feet—a boy and a girl.

Fig. 13: Introducing Ignorance and Want.

The girl has Scrooge's eyes, which must have been an intentional effect. She looks up at him, as we've watched him look up at so many others since his oneiric journey commenced. Beseeching eyes of ocularly animated desperation. And eyes that make a plea for help. Scrooge continues with his ace investigative reporting, asking the ghost if the children belong to him. The boy is Ignorance, the girl is Want, he is told. And they belong to all of mankind.

We were not prepared for an image that doubles as revelation. The nameless boy and the nameless girl are like all of us—requiring fellowship, and if not an actual protector, the knowledge that one could count on a fellow human when in need. They sit on the snow, and have clearly been crying, shades of the homeless woman with her newborn child when the ghost of Jacob Marley flew off into the night. The image of the ghost and the children recalls Goya's Black Paintings, but as though one of those canvases had been trepanned, drained of the scant colors it possessed. Fittingly, Scrooge's face is blanched, having become whiter than the snow beneath his feet.

The ghost and mankind's progeny dissolve, with the voice of the former booming, repeating Scrooge's words spoken earlier ("Are there no prisons? Are there no workhouses?") to the alms collectors who had called at his counting house. Scrooge is stranded, left in the street, his hands pressed over his ears to try and cope with the ghost's departing volume.

Hands are vital in *Scrooge*, as they were for the departing Keats, because they are the symbols of connection and guidance. Of leadership and assistance. They are the physical tools of steadying someone else. Hurst cuts to a shot where Scrooge is further down the street, his back to the foreground of the composition, and to us, and to what draws near. It's another deep focus shot. The snow-covered street is a passageway down which one must venture. There's no other road or passage. The London alleyway as metaphor for Robert Frost's dictum of "the only way out is through."

A trave of light stretches over Scrooge's head and through his torso. His arms are not visible. He turns to run, because he has to go somewhere. The words of the Ghost of Christmas Present have modulated into clangorous laughter. And as Scrooge runs—towards the camera and us—he is halted by a hand. Nothing else. No body, no head, just a hand that presents itself at the edge of the frame. Scrooge slides on the snow, and all but crashes into this hand, his mouth agog, a burbling sound—as if he's shred his larynx—coming from the back of his throat.

***

There was a town in which I used to live, where I hope to live again. It was a place I loved, which I lost. Where I lost a lot of my life, and a lot of myself. A few years after my losses, at Christmastime, I returned to this town, renting a room at an inn, so I could be back there once more. Not fully reclaim what I had lost—but reclamation is a process. One starts by trying to make a dent in it. But you could say that this was my Christmas present—at the time—and also my Christmas yet to come. Where I wanted my future Christmases to be spent, though in a home rather than an inn.

On Christmas Eve morning I went for a run, encountering a woman walking her dog who had not lived in the town long. She told me about her family, asked about me. I told her where I had come from, why I was staying at the inn that was across the street from her home. Even if I was someone who forgets much, I would always remember what she said to me. "Colin, you look like you've come to a place to try and put your soul back together again." That night I could not sleep. I replayed the past. I feared for the future. I put on the television, despite the inn having only ten or twelve channels, and there it was again: *Scrooge*, only later in the film, when a hand halts a man in a road—a man trying to put his soul back together. And I sat up, and I watched.

Encountering *Scrooge* in the middle of the night, as I've had a propensity to do during my life, is not hard to do. The film was released in America as *A Christmas Carol*, on Halloween, 1951. The distributors knew what they were doing. *Scrooge* is more horror film than cinematic stocking stuffer. A contemporaneous *New York Times* review called Sim a "crabbed creature"—fair enough—and commended Ernest Thesiger as the perfect undertaker, but the piece was careful to issue a word of warning.

"Take heed on one point," the reviewer wrote, going on to state that the 1938 version—which has always been what I think of as the daytime version of *A Christmas Carol*—isn't a work that prepares you for this one, with "Its nightmare conceits and shuddering horror." The *Times* reviewer conceded that this was no holiday affair. "The usual conceptions of Christmas in terms of pudding and flowing bowls are not visualized in this picture to any conspicuous degree." Addinsell's score is "full of interpolations of familiar Christmas songs," with "heavy discords and harsh sounds of misery." More than anything, *Scrooge* "is an accurate comprehension of the agony of a shabby soul."[6]

Well said. Often when we look back on old reviews, they're wide of the mark to baffling degrees. I'm not sure you can fail to understand—and feel—what *Scrooge* is, though. Viewers often found it too dark, not Christmas-y enough, and the film became a midnight movie. Not as a piece of camp, but rather that's when you often caught it on the television. *Scrooge* is a TV movie, which is different than a made-for-TV movie. I like that almost all of us who have experienced *Scrooge* have done so in homes, and often late at night, when it is harder not to be honest with one's self. Your late-night-iteration is the target demo for *Scrooge*, just as it was for the man played by Alastair Sim.

The Ghost of Christmas Yet to Come doesn't speak, and wears a cowl that we associate with the Reaper. Scrooge seems to think he may die, but he asks this ghost to lead him. He's going through, in the Frostian sense, no matter what the cost.

There are scenes of a grieving Cratchit home, now that Tiny Tim has died. It's a home of darkness. The rosy light of the Christmas meal is all but abrogated. We could be inside of Van Gogh's *The Potato Eaters*. The following sequence is also a Noel Langley creation. Mrs. Dilber and Scrooge's laundress (Louise Hampton) enter the pawn shop of Old Joe (Miles Malleson). Mrs. Dilber has nicked some dead fellow's bedsheets and curtains, plus some clothes, and now she wants to sell them. Scrooge is in denial as he looks on. He must know that these items belong to him, but it's not every day you watch how someone would handle your stuff and speak about you after you're dead. Mrs. Dilber has betrayed Scrooge, but also not really—again, the duality. What should have happened? The curtains would have been discarded anyway. Might as well get a few coins put in the purse instead. The undertaker Mr. Stretch arrives, and what a crew this is. The scene is not short, either. Hurst puts our noses in the mess. Mr. Stretch has the real goodies—buttons, watch, fob, pencil case, broach.

Scrooge is a film of returning. Scrooge has returned to his past, to his bed. Jacob Marley has returned. The audience returns to the first scene of the movie, as the Ghost of Christmas Yet to Come next shows Scrooge the inside of the trading exchange, where the men who had once greeted him with a sarcastic "Happy Christmas"—knowing his feelings on the subject—discuss the merit in attending a particular dead man's funeral. The consensus: it's worth going if there's a free lunch.

Scrooge asks the ghost whose funeral was being discussed, but again he knows. It's an overlooked point, but Scrooge is doubtless noting that these people—Bob Cratchit, Mrs. Dilber, the trading exchange guys—don't look that much different or older than when he saw them last. The insinuation is that Scrooge is not long for the world, as he has been going in it.

Another dissolve and we're in a graveyard out of German Expressionism 101. Touch was a requirement of traveling with the other ghosts. Nearness. Not so with our Reaper fellow. Scrooge follows a number of paces back, and the ghost leads by pointing—again, the hand. But is the hand living or dead? Is it both, and a man like Scrooge has a say in which side prevails?

Seeing his own headstone, Scrooge begs for his life, weeping, desperate, but with words that are controlled and accurate. It's Sim in classic Sim elocution mode. On his knees, he looks up to the ghost, and Scrooge's hands, clenched as if in prayer, but a prayer for the human, rather than holy, spirit—touch the hand of the specter. "I'm not the man I was," Scrooge says. He both is and he is not. A person is comprised, in part, of their past, their choices. They do not go away. And Scrooge's past and choices remain with him. But Scrooge is also not who he was, because for the first time, he is something new—actually living. The living hand. In human form.

***

As *Scrooge* is an undertaking of returning, the eponymous hero—and let us bestow hero status upon him—of Brian Desmond Hurst's one masterpiece, awakens once more in his bed, at home, different than he was the time before. I'm not sure there's a better goal to life: to return once more to the home, changed for the better than when you last left. Rinse and repeat, as they say, day upon day.

Scrooge awakens to find Mrs. Dilber in his rooms, and as we've seen, he freaks her out with his dance of joy (much darting) as tuneful bells—the antithesis of Jacob Marley's carillon-of-death entrance—play in the church steeples high above the lanes outside.

Scrooge charms Mrs. Dilber, quintuples her pay, orders a Christmas goose for the Cratchits. But there is one scene in particular that makes the horror of this work of art complete, because it provides release. The payoff of the horror can take myriad forms. The payoff may be death, it can be the monster at last revealed, the vampire defeated. The payoff of horror for *Scrooge* occurs at the home of Nephew Fred. We know what Scrooge looks like when he's scared. We've seen it dozens of times. And we see it one last time, but this is good fear, the cherishable fear.

He arrives at Fred's house, with the snow falling, as the melody of "Barbara Allen" plays. It was with the death of his sister—and the birth of his nephew—that Scrooge became what Dickens termed a haunted man, in another Christmas story, one that Vincent Van Gogh re-read every holiday season, after his own family had cast him out. Fred's maid opens the door, and she's shocked by whom she finds standing on the other side. Presumably she's never met Scrooge, but she's heard so much about him that she knows who this is.

Theresa Derrington plays the maid. Virtually no one knew who acted in the part for many decades. It's as small a part as there is in the entire film, but beloved by all who have taken this journey with Scrooge, because she embodies what this new man wishes to be, whom he wants to live as.

She doesn't know him, but he needs her. He enters the home, where Fred and his guests are singing "Barbara Allen." We've only heard the melody up until now. Hurst and Addinsell have saved the words for this moment. They are giving us our release, as Scrooge has had his.

The maid has the same doe-like eyes as Scrooge. They fit together, these two humans who do not know each other. Scrooge looks increasingly distressed with each layer of winter clothing that he removes, to be hung up on the coat rack, because when the last layer is gone, he'll have to enter the room with the revelers. He stops at the door leading into this room. He can go no further. He turns to the maid, and she helps him. A smile, a nod of support. That is all it takes, and everything that it takes.

Into this place of happiness and warmth the former miser goes, the music coming to an abrupt halt, but note where it stops: just before the singing of the line, "Young man, I think you're dying."

No one knows what to say. Is Scrooge in his cups? But Fred knows exactly what to do—he's that kind of person—and rises to welcome his uncle. Fred is pretty stoked—he's thrilled to have Scrooge in the house. Fred's wife isn't sure what to think, so Scrooge walks over to her—strings playing the "Barbara Allen" melody—and offers an apology. "Can you forgive a pigheaded old fool for having no eyes to see with, no ears to hear with, for all of these years?"

Heavy atmosphere in this room, yes? Scrooge is given another assistance once more by someone who is a stranger to him, and yet provides a good turn, looks out for him. Our hale and hearty Mr. Tupper calls for a polka—sotto voce, not drawing any attention to himself, because this is not his moment on which to intrude. And with that, Scrooge dances with Fred's wife, and boy does he dance. Up and down the room, a life force of movement. A true darter.

Fig. 14: Post-haunted. Life begins.

Marley's ghost had lamented an inability to intercede in the lives of those needing intercession, but in this scene, I always think of how that's not really true, because of what we are watching as the audience, and what Scrooge is doing in the film; what he's become, what he is, as we leave him.

The living hand—and the living hand of art—always reaches us, when we are reachable. May we all endeavor, no matter the horrors with which we contend—and the horrors that help us, and make us feel alive—to be thus blessed, and thus so.

FOOTNOTES

6. Crowther, Bosley, *The New York Times*, November 29, 1951.

DEVIL'S ADVOCATES

"Auteur Publishing's new Devil's Advocates critiques on individual titles offer bracingly fresh perspectives from passionate writers. The series will perfectly complement the BFI archive volumes." Christopher Fowler, Independent on Sunday

DEAD OF NIGHT – JEZ CONOLLY & DAVID BATES

Dead of Night *featured contributions from some of the finest directors, writers and technicians ever to work in British film. This is the first time a single book has been dedicated to its analysis. and includes a selection of rarely seen designs produced by the film's production designer, Michael Relph.*

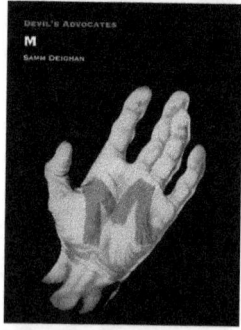

M – SAMM DEIGHAN

Samm Deighan explores the way Fritz Lang uses horror and thriller tropes in M, *particularly in terms of how it functions as a bridge between German Expressionism and Hollywood's growing fixation on sympathetic killers in the '40s.*

THE MUMMY – DORIS V. SUTHERLAND

"This monograph serves as an excellent starting point for those wishing to research this film... As well as more general issues such as the ghost/horror genre, representations of imperialism, sexism and xenophobia... The clear structure and concise language make it accessible to the casual reader as well as the academic researcher." Tina Stockman, Media Education Journal